Acknowledgements

The authors and publishers acknowledge the following sources of copyright material and are grateful for the permissions granted. While every effort has been made, it has not always been possible to identify the sources of all the material used, or to trace all copyright holders. If any omissions are brought to our notice we will be happy to include the appropriate acknowledgement on reprinting.

Kathryn M. Borg / *The Sunday Times of Malta* for 'Educating children through sport' (page 52), © Kathryn M. Borg 2003.

Claudia Dreifus for 'Congo's reclusive forest creatures' (page 20).

The Daily Telegraph Magazine for 'Frozen in time' by Julius Strauss (page 72), © Telegraph Media Group Limited 2005.

Guardian Newspapers Ltd for 'In a class of their own' by Randeep Ramesh (page 58), © Guardian News & Media Limited 2006, and 'King of the chatroom' by Peter Kingston (page 42), © Guardian News and Media Limited 2004.

Nicholas Farrell for 'Zest for life' (page 24).

Illustrations by John Dillow (Beehive Illustration) (pages 18, 60, 76) and David Woodroffe (pages 20, 52)

The FAIRTRADE Mark (page 26) by permission of the Fairtrade Foundation

Photographs by permission of Apex News & Pictures (page 68), Corbis Images UK, Ltd (pages 24, 36, 40, 72), Getty Images (page 20) and OSF Oxford Scientific (page 74)
Cover image: © Pic and Mix Images/Alamy

Practice Tests for IGCSE English as a Second Language

Reading and Writing

Book 2

Previously published by Georgian Press

Marian Barry,
Barbara Campbell,
Sue Daish

CAMBRIDGE
UNIVERSITY PRESS

University Printing House, Cambridge CB2 8BS, United Kingdom

Cambridge University Press is part of the University of Cambridge.

It furthers the University's mission by disseminating knowledge in the pursuit of education, learning and research at the highest international levels of excellence.

www.cambridge.org
Information on this title: www.cambridge.org/9780521140645 (without key)
www.cambridge.org/9780521140652 (with key)

First published by Georgian Press (Jersey) Limited 2007
Reprinted and published by Cambridge University Press 2010
7th printing 2014

A catalogue record for this publication is available from the British Library

ISBN 978-0-521-14064-5 Paperback without key
ISBN 978-0-521-14065-2 Paperback with key

Produced by AMR Design Ltd (www.amrdesign.com)

Cover image: © Pic and Mix Images/Alamy

Contents

IGCSE IN E2L AT A GLANCE

PAPER 1 Reading and Writing

(Core curriculum) $1\frac{1}{2}$ hours

PAPER 2 Reading and Writing

(Extended curriculum) 2 hours

EXERCISE 1: READING

Candidates answer questions of factual detail about a text (an advertisement, brochure, leaflet, guide, instructions, etc). Skimming/scanning and gist reading skills are tested, and short answers using single words or phrases are required.

Total marks: Core 6, Extended 8

EXERCISE 2: READING

Candidates answer questions requiring a more detailed understanding of a text, such as a report or newspaper/magazine article with a graphical element (a map, chart, graph or diagram). One question may ask candidates to make a list of points based on the text.

Total marks: Core 10, Extended 14

EXERCISE 3: INFORMATION TRANSFER

Candidates complete a form or skeletal notes using information given in a scenario on the question paper.

Total marks: Core 10, Extended 8

EXERCISE 4: NOTE-MAKING

Candidates write brief notes from a written text, under a heading or headings provided.

Total marks: Core 6, Extended 8

EXERCISE 5: SUMMARY WRITING

Extended candidates write about 100 words on an aspect or aspects of a written text, such as a newspaper or magazine article.

Core candidates write a paragraph of no more than 70 words, using their notes from Exercise 4.

Total marks: Core 4, Extended 10

EXERCISE 6: WRITING

Extended candidates write about 150–200 words (Core candidates 100–150 words) of continuous prose. The purpose, format and audience are specified, e.g. an informal letter to a friend, or an article about a holiday for the school magazine. Candidates must use an appropriate style and register. A stimulus is provided, in the form of pictures or photos and/or short prompts.

Total marks: Core 10, Extended 18

EXERCISE 7: WRITING

Extended candidates write about 150–200 words (Core candidates 100–150 words) of continuous prose. The format, purpose and audience are specified, and will be different from Exercise 6, e.g. a formal letter to a newspaper about a local issue. Candidates must use an appropriate style and register. A stimulus is provided, in the form of pictures or photos and/or short prompts.

The prompts are a guide to help students focus their thoughts and are not meant to be prescriptive. Good candidates can use them selectively, and some may choose to write totally without reference to the prompts. This is perfectly acceptable, as long as they do not drift away from the point of the question.

Total marks: Core 10, Extended 18

TOTAL MARKS FOR PAPER 1: 56
Weighting: 70% **Grades available:** C–G

TOTAL MARKS FOR PAPER 2: 84
Weighting: 70% **Grades available:** A–E

PAPER 3 Listening

(Core curriculum) 30–40 minutes

PAPER 4 Listening

(Extended curriculum) 45 minutes

QUESTIONS 1–6

Candidates answer questions on six short spoken texts, such as informal conversations, travel announcements, answerphone messages. They are required to identify specific points of information. Each text is heard twice, and short answers (one word or phrase) are required.

Total marks: Core 7, Extended 8

QUESTIONS 7 AND 8

Candidates listen to two recordings of longer spoken texts, such as formal or informal conversations, interviews, monologues, formal talks. Each text is heard twice.

Candidates fill in skeletal notes or close gaps on forms or charts with single words or short phrases. They need to be able to select information from what may be incidental.

Total marks: Core 12, Extended 16

QUESTIONS 9 AND 10

Candidates listen to two recordings, which may be informal conversations or more formal talks, interviews, etc. Each text is heard twice.

Extended candidates answer about six questions on each recording, requiring short or sentence-length answers. Core candidates answer about 10 true-false or multiple-choice questions on each recording by ticking boxes. In both cases, candidates need to be able to understand more complex meanings, opinions and attitudes of the speakers. Extended candidates should also be able to infer meaning implicit in the text.

Total marks: Core 11, Extended 12

TOTAL MARKS FOR PAPER 3: 30
Weighting: 30% **Grades available:** C–G

TOTAL MARKS FOR PAPER 4: 36
Weighting: 30% **Grades available:** A–E

COMPONENT 5 Oral test

(Core and Extended curriculum) 10–12 mins

Candidates take part in a discussion with the teacher/examiner, and possibly another candidate, on a set topic. There are up to five topics, e.g. holidays, health and fitness, the rights and wrongs of zoos, winning the lottery. After a short warm-up, which is not assessed, candidates are allowed 2-3 minutes to read the Oral Assessment card which has been selected by the examiner. The cards include prompts to guide the discussion. Candidates are not allowed to make written notes.

The conversation itself should last 6-9 minutes.

Detailed guidance is provided by CIE on how to conduct the Oral tests, and advice should be sought regarding all aspects of the tests.

Grades available: 1 (high) to 5 (low)

COMPONENT 6 Oral coursework

(Core and Extended curriculum)

Instead of Component 5, centres may, with the permission of CIE, opt for Component 6. This is a coursework option in which oral work is set and assessed by the teacher, at any time in the year before the written exam. Each candidate is assessed on three oral tasks, e.g. role play situations, telephone conversations, interviews, paired or group discussions, brief talks followed by discussion, debates. Further guidance on suitable types of tasks is given in the Distance Training Pack, available from CIE.

Grades available: 1 (high) to 5 (low)

More detailed information about the IGCSE in E2L examination, including support available for teachers, can be obtained from University of Cambridge International Examinations, 1 Hills Road, Cambridge CB1 2EU, United Kingdom, and online at **www.cie.org.uk**

About the IGCSE in E2L

These Practice Tests are designed to give practice in the Reading and Writing papers of the revised (2006) Cambridge IGCSE examination in English as Second Language. The exam is set at two levels, known as Core and Extended. The Core papers are aimed at lower-intermediate to intermediate students, hoping to achieve a grade C–G, while the Extended level is for intermediate to upper-intermediate students hoping to achieve grades A*–E. (See *IGCSE in E2L at a Glance* on pages 4/5 for a detailed overview.)

The exam is usually taken as part of the IGCSE curriculum, which offers a wide range of subjects. It can be taken at any age, although most students are about 16 years old. Students generally study for the exam over a period of two years, which allows them to develop both intellectually and emotionally.

The IGCSE in E2L qualification is widely recognised by universities where evidence of attainment in English is a requirement of entry.

About the Practice Tests

Like the exam, the material used in the Practice Tests aims to be international in perspective, culturally fair to students from all parts of the world, educational in impact and to reflect the needs and interests of teenagers. Exam tasks are realistic and similar to what students could be expected to meet at work, in training or in academic study.

The **Practice Tests** have the following benefits:

- They introduce students to the exam format.
- They allow students to experience a simulated exam under exam-type conditions.
- They help to build confidence and to develop exam techniques.
- Gaps in students' learning and skills can be uncovered and remedied.
- Students can acquire insight into what the examiners are looking for.

Common questions asked about the IGCSE in E2L

Why are there two choices of entry level?

The separate papers for Core and Extended levels are intended to encompass a wide ability range and to allow all students a chance of being awarded a qualification and a grade which reflects their level of ability in English.

This book contains four Extended-level Practice Tests (the most popular level).

What are the differences between Papers 1 and 2? (i.e. Reading and Writing, Core, and Reading and Writing, Extended)

The exercises and tasks for the two levels are very similar. The differences are largely in the way the same exercises are adapted to be more challenging at Extended level and to stretch the candidates further. This is achieved mainly by asking additional questions on a reading text or by asking Extended candidates to write at greater length. However, there are a few specific differences. At Core level, note-taking and summary tasks are based on one text, whereas at Extended level, two different texts are used and the tasks are kept completely separate.

Some of the exam-type texts look very demanding. Is this a real problem?
Although some exam-type texts are demanding in terms of reading level, the tasks which students are asked to carry out in the exam are very straightforward. Exam practice will build the necessary confidence required to tackle difficult-looking texts with assurance.

I notice there is no Use of English paper in the exam. Why is this?
The aim of the exam is to enable students to make the language that they know work effectively in a practical context. The testing of language structures and vocabulary is integrated into the assessment of students' ability to carry out practical communication tasks. A few slight technical mistakes will not affect a student's grade as long as the overall impression is appropriate. This approach is fairer to students learning English in a second-language situation, where they may be 'picking up' English in a number of ways, not just learning it in their English classes.

How to use the Practice Tests

The Tests are designed to be used as flexibly as possible. They can be introduced at any time in the learning process when you feel students will benefit from being tested on exam-style exercises. Tests may be broken down into stand-alone exercises and integrated into coursework, perhaps as consolidation for work on a particular skill. Some exercises could be discussed in class before students start work on them; others could be treated as a check on skill level and students asked to complete them without help. The latter approach is also useful for diagnostic assessment at the start of the course. Alternatively, a whole test could be taken as a mock exam under exam conditions when you feel the students are ready. Obviously, you may have to extend normal lesson time to do this. Test results should help predict the kind of grade the students will get in the exam itself.

Timing

One of the benefits of Practice Tests is that students have the opportunity to practise timing themselves to see how they can build up speed for the actual exam. You can help them do this by gradually reducing the amount of time you allocate to particular exercises. This will encourage them to sustain concentration at a higher level for longer periods, to read and retain information more effectively, and to produce writing of a better and more consistent quality.

General advice on marking

When you decide on a mark, you need to take into account how well the student has completed the particular task. Students who fulfil a task very effectively should be given either full or very high marks. Students who do less well should naturally be awarded lower marks. However, the extent to which you apply this criterion will depend on the needs and capabilities of your own students. In order to motivate and encourage, you may want to be quite lenient in grading work at first, when the exercises are relatively unfamiliar, and become stricter as students progress in skills and experience.

Marking comprehension exercises

The right answer to a comprehension question is one in which the student has extracted the correct information from the text. An answer to a question may also be drawn from non-verbal information such as a chart or graph.

Sometimes there is more than one possible answer to a question. This is shown in the Key by the use of slash/slashes. Information which may be included in the answer but which is not necessary for achieving the mark is put into brackets. Answers requiring specific amounts, percentages, numbers, etc must be exact, not generalised. Sometimes an answer to a question has more than one element and both elements are required to obtain the mark. This is shown clearly both in the layout of the question and in the Key.

Marking information transfer (form-filling) exercises

Look out for the most common exam mistakes, which are:

- Filling in the form for themselves, not the person in the scenario.
- Mistakes in copying factual details (e.g. names, addresses, telephone numbers, dates), which need to be error-free to obtain the marks allocated.
- Not using block capital letters where required.
- Not following specific instructions such as *Circle*, *Delete*, *Tick*, etc.

Marking note-taking exercises

In the exam, the note-taking exercises take the form of headings followed by bullet points, against which students write their notes. Full sentences are not required and answers can be one word or a brief phrase. Students should take care with spelling, however, as they may inadvertently miss a mark if a misspelled word gives another meaning. The bullet points guide the student as to the number of points to find, and each point should be used only once.

Weak note-taking answers tend to extract irrelevant information from the text or put the right points under the wrong headings.

Marking summaries

Summary questions are selective which means that only some of the information in the text is relevant.

Core-level summaries are linked to the preceding note-taking task. Students are asked to re-present their notes in continuous prose. For example, in Exercise 4 the students may make notes for a wildlife club on a text about endangered species. Then, in Exercise 5, they have to summarise the notes into a connected paragraph for a school magazine feature. The summary exercise for Extended-level is completely separate from the preceding note-taking exercise.

When marking summaries look for the following:

- Inclusion of the appropriate content points.
- The ability to change some of the language of the text into own words without destroying the original meaning.
- Use of a clear and logical sequence.
- Good spelling, grammar and punctuation.

Good summaries should be completely understandable, even by someone who has not seen the original text. Weaker summaries, on the other hand, show less understanding of the task by failing to include all the relevant points. Weaker answers often include information which is not required by the question, chunks of text are copied, and there are errors in grammar and vocabulary which obscure the meaning.

Detailed guidelines for marking the language aspect of the summary exercises are given on page 82 of the Key.

Marking compositions

Exam compositions are not marked by examiners with perfect model answers next to them. They mark each script on its own merits and in accordance with an agreed interpretation of exam guidelines. (These are summarised in the table provided on page 83 of the Key.) When marking your own students' work, you can grade it appropriately and help them reach exam standards by using the following approach.

Firstly, a balanced view of a composition is important when you decide on an overall mark. One or two errors should not 'ruin' an effective piece of work if these are balanced out by other strengths. At IGCSE level, even the best students are expected to suffer from some frustration with the language and to make one or two mistakes, especially if they are being ambitious in their choice of grammar, vocabulary and idioms.

The best compositions, as a rule of thumb, are clear, straightforward and easy to read. They have definite beginnings and endings. The student shows involvement with the topic he/she is writing about, and is able to arouse your interest in it. Compositions of this kind can be given marks at the top end of the range.

Weak writing, on the other hand, is much more difficult to follow and you may find yourself re-reading it several times in order to make out the sense. As a reader, you don't feel drawn into the topic. After you have finished reading it, you may not be entirely clear about the meaning, or the student's opinions, or, if he/she was telling you a story, what exactly happened or how the story ended. Weak writing should be given marks at the lower end of the range.

Some writing is neither very good nor very weak. The task is interpreted in a safe but unexciting way. The meaning is clear but as a reader, you won't find it especially interesting or enjoyable to read. Average compositions of this type can be given middle-range marks.

Checklist for marking

In addition to the general guidance given above, you may like to use this checklist to help you when selecting a mark for your students' work.

1 ***Answering the question***
Does the writing cover the question set, or does it drift away from the question? If rubric prompts are given, are these addressed?

2 ***Sentence construction***
Do sentences begin and end in the right places? How varied are the sentences – are they a mixture of lengths or mostly short and simple? Are any relative clauses used?

3 Grammar
To what extent are tenses, modal verbs, conditionals and other grammatical features accurate where used? Is there some ambition in the use of grammatical structures, or does the student keep to very simple structures he/she can manage accurately?

4 Vocabulary
How varied and accurate is the vocabulary for the intended meaning? Does the student keep to limited and repetitive vocabulary, or is he/she making a real effort to use a wider range of vocabulary? Are any idioms used?

5 Punctuation
Is punctuation used? Is the punctuation accurate? Has the candidate set him/herself a more complex punctuation task (e.g. punctuating direct speech), and how well is this task achieved?

6 Spelling
How accurate is the spelling? Are simple, common words (e.g. *house, table*) spelled correctly? Are misspellings mostly because the student is trying to achieve a more ambitious effect with complex vocabulary? Are the spelling mistakes phonetic (e.g. *frend* for *friend*)? Remember, phonetic mistakes interfere less with communication than other kinds of spelling errors.

7 Paragraphing
Has the student organised his/her own work into paragraphs? Are the paragraphs in the right sequence and accurately linked together so the writing makes a coherent whole?

8 Subject matter
How well does the student deal with the topic? Does he/she get straight into the topic and seem interested in it, and also make the reader interested in it?

9 Tone, register, sense of audience
Do the tone, register and sense of audience feel right for the purpose? Competition entries, for example, should sound positive, enthusiastic and encouraging; a letter to a friend should sound friendly and sympathetic, whereas a letter to a newspaper should sound more formal and distanced.

10 Sense of argument
Is the argument set out clearly and logically and does the writer come to a clear conclusion? Are you sure what he/she thinks, or are there contradictions? Does the writer give clear examples? Are linking words (e.g. *however, moreover*) used, and do these help to make the meaning clear?

11 Length of work
Is the writing about the right length, within the word limit given?

Helping students improve their work

Setting and marking work is a tried and tested way of supporting learning. There are several ways of marking work so that students can learn and move on from their mistakes. Marking is most helpful when it is selective, so that some errors are highlighted and others are overlooked.

Error analysis

Error analysis is used to draw the attention of the class to an extract written by a fellow student which is a clear example of a mistake to avoid. You can read the extract aloud and ask students to analyse the error(s), or write the extract on the board. If your class is not familiar with error analysis, it is useful to explain the idea behind it so that the student who wrote the extract understands that the criticism is objective. Error analysis is a particularly useful way of giving feedback if you come across an example of something which has recently been taught to the class, e.g. an error in tone and register, or an inappropriate beginning or ending, or a point of grammar. It is best to focus the error analysis on a few sentences extracted from a student's composition, rather than looking at a whole piece of work.

Written feedback

In addition to error analysis, you can write comments at the end of students' work. The most helpful ones are usually specific comments that pick up on areas of language that have recently been taught. You can ask students to rewrite drafts of work to produce a better example. Misspelled words should be written out correctly for students to copy and learn. Areas of improvement should also be commented on and praised, to reinforce students' sense of progress and to continue to motivate and encourage.

When facing an exam, many students naturally feel a little nervous. The information and advice below should help resolve your worries and enable you to do your best. Remember, lots of practice and hard work are the most important thing, so keep at it! You'll probably do much better than you think!

Paper 1, Reading and Writing (Core level)

The Core paper has seven exercises and must be completed in 90 minutes. There are two comprehension exercises, a form-filling exercise, a note-taking exercise with a linked summary exercise, and two composition questions. See the chart on pages 4/5 for more information.

Paper 2, Reading and Writing (Extended level)

The Extended paper has seven exercises and must be completed in two hours. There are two comprehension exercises (the second exercise may include finding a list of points), a form-filling exercise, a note-taking exercise, a summary exercise and two composition exercises. See the chart on pages 4/5 for more information.

Exercises 1 and 2 (Reading)

Exercise 1 is based on a brochure or advertisement with straightforward questions. Exercise 2 is based on a newspaper or magazine article and the information given in the text is more detailed. The way to do well in both exercises is to be as alert as possible to all the clues, to read quickly but with a lot of concentration, and to take care over the detail of the questions. For example, pictures/diagrams or headings supplied will give clues to meaning. Ask yourself: where is this text from and what is it likely to be about?

When reading, don't worry too much about words you don't understand – try to work them out from context. If you still don't understand, don't worry. Understanding them may not be necessary in order to give the right answer.

The questions often use different words and phrases to those given in the text because the exam is looking for understanding of meaning, not just matching words together. Find evidence for the answer by checking the text. Answer everything. You may get the answer right, even if you are not sure! The right answer to a question is one which contains the correct information, which can often be copied from the text. Answers can be very brief – a single word may be enough.

If you are asked a question such as *How much...?/How many...?/How long...?* requiring information about measurements, times, costs, percentages, etc, your answer must be specific. For example: *2 hours 10 minutes* (NOT *about 2 hours*), *The trip costs $149.50* (NOT *about $150*), *Five out of six houses* (NOT *Most houses*).

The questions usually follow the sequence of the text. For example, the answer to question (b) will be found at an earlier point in the text than the answer to question (c). Some questions have two bits to them. In this case, make sure you find answers to both bits of the question.

Exercise 2 may have a final question asking you to write a list of points. You can find the points by scanning the text and copying out the right information.

The number of marks allocated to each question is shown in brackets at the end of the question.

Exercise 3 (Form-filling)

This is an 'information transfer' exercise, which means you have to complete a form or set of notes based on information given. The key to doing really well in this exercise is to be careful with the detail and to check your work. You can get a lot of easy marks just by making sure facts such as names, addresses and telephone numbers are copied exactly. It's important that you spell everything correctly.

Exercise 4 (Note-taking)

Exercise 4 is not particularly hard because headings for the notes are given, and bullet points are supplied to guide your answers. Remember, each heading requires different bits of information from the text. Don't repeat anything you write or add any ideas or opinions of your own – everything has to come from the text. And remember that the finished notes should make sense! When practising, it's worth asking yourself: could someone reading these notes understand them even if they hadn't seen the original passage?

Exercise 5 (Summary)

In Exercise 5 you have to write a summary based on a text. In Paper 1, the exercise is linked to the notes for Exercise 4. All you need to do in this case is produce a clear paragraph in full sentences, reworking the notes you have already made and using some words of your own.

Extended candidates should read the text for their summary quickly and underline any relevant sections. Check back with the summary question. Join the ideas you have picked out into one or more coherent paragraphs, using some words and phrases of your own. Check back quickly again with the question and make any changes. Count the number of words. If you have time, make another draft of your summary, incorporating any changes. If you don't have time, simply make corrections to the first draft. In the exam itself, don't worry about the summary looking 'messy' as long as it is easily readable.

Make sure you read the question carefully because sometimes you are asked to include more than one aspect of the text in your summary.

Exercises 6 and 7 (Composition writing)

You need to do one task for each of these exercises. Typical tasks are writing a short formal or informal letter, or an article for the school magazine or a newspaper. In Exercise 7, prompts in the form of imaginary comments are usually given to help you understand the type of situation and to give you ideas. The key to starting well in the composition is to make sure you understand the situation, so give a little thought to what it's about before writing.

If you use the prompts in your composition, be selective (don't try to use them all), and expand them with reasons and examples. Don't just copy out the prompts, though – you won't get marks for copying. If you don't like the prompts, don't use them. You can write a good letter or article without any of them. Just check that your composition is still relevant to the question.

General advice on writing

The main point to remember is that the examiner is marking positively, looking for ways to reward you, not trying to criticise, so try to show the best you can do.

One or two mistakes in grammar or spelling won't 'spoil' your work if the overall impression is good. Try to remember the following points:

- It's worth trying to **be a little ambitious** in your writing. Take one or two small risks to make your writing more interesting by using more complex structures or more unusual vocabulary. This can get a higher mark than sticking with safe but simple work.
- Let your personality shine through in your writing. The examiner will reward this. **Ideas and examples from your own life** are interesting to the examiner, even if you don't think so! Background details about your own life, family and school, and personal views which are relevant to the question, really help in gaining higher marks.
- **Plan before you write**. Think and plan in paragraphs. Three paragraphs are usually enough.
- **Keep to the point of the question, and cover all parts** – don't drift away and begin to write in general terms, and don't ignore any part of the question.
- **Take care** with grammar, spelling, vocabulary, punctuation and paragraphing. Indicate where paragraphs should be by putting // if you forget to write in paragraphs.
- **Proofread your work** at the end and correct careless mistakes.
- Have a **clear opening and closing sentence**. Examples:
  Formal letters
  I am interested in applying for...
  I was concerned to hear/read about...
  I look forward to hearing from you soon.
  I hope we will be able to arrange a meeting soon.
  Informal letters
  Just a quick line to tell you about Danielle's wedding.
  You'll be surprised when I tell you what happened to me last week!
  I must end now as I've got to catch up on my homework.
  It'll be great to see you next month. Give my love to everyone in the family.
- Use a **suitable tone and register**. For informal writing, instead of writing to an imaginary person such as Bill or Mary, it helps to think of someone you actually know (Ahmed? Pedro? Martina?) and to write to him or her. This will help to achieve a more natural tone and register.
  Sounding positive and enthusiastic makes a good impression and is the required tone for a competition entry. Balance negative ideas with positive points.
- Show **awareness of your audience** – a close friend, someone you haven't met before, a teenage magazine, a school newsletter, etc. Useful phrases for showing audience awareness are:
  I don't usually write to newspapers/the school magazine but I feel strongly about...
  My class has become involved in a really interesting project about...
  I think our school should...
  People of my age often feel...
  Do write back. I'd love to hear your views. (for the school magazine)
  I'd be very interested in hearing what other readers think. (for a newspaper)

Advice on time management

You'll probably find some exercises easy and others more challenging. Common sense in planning your time is your best aid. Core candidates have just under 13 minutes per exercise, but the exercises are not equal in difficulty and the marks given to them reflect this. Extended candidates have just over 17 minutes per exercise. Again, the exercises are not equally complex, so adjust the amount of time you spend, depending on how easy you find an exercise.

Think in minutes rather than parts of an hour – minutes do count and will add up. Keep a close eye on the clock. The longer you spend on one question, the less time you have for another. Don't spend too long on any one question – it's not worth it.

Don't count your words in the writing section. This is not necessary and, if you have practised, you will know what 150 or 200 words look like in your handwriting. Lined paper is provided in the exam as a guideline to the length required.

Exercise 1 is the 'easiest', but you don't have to start with the first exercise on the paper. Start wherever you feel comfortable and most confident. Don't forget about an exercise altogether, though!

This book will be very helpful because you can practise answering questions according to the time limit. Lots of practice really does make a big difference to speed and confidence. Be generous with yourself at first, then reduce the amount of time you allow yourself as your skills increase.

And finally...

We hope you enjoy using these Practice Tests, make lots of progress and achieve the success you are hoping for. Good luck!

PRACTICE TEST 1

Exercise 1

Read the following information about a Roman fort, and then answer the questions on the opposite page.

ARBEIA ROMAN FORT AND MUSEUM

LOCATION AND HISTORY

Arbeia Roman Fort is situated on Hadrian's Wall. This mighty frontier system was the most important structure built by the Romans in Britain, and it has now been designated a World Heritage Site. In AD 122 the Emperor Hadrian ordered the wall to be built across northern Britain, from coast to coast.

Overlooking the mouth of the River Tyne and built around AD 160, Arbeia Fort was the military supply base for the soldiers who were stationed in the seventeen forts along Hadrian's Wall.

The fort has been gradually excavated to reveal its secrets and to show what life was really like in Roman Britain. Some original parts have been revealed, and there are spectacular reconstructions that show how Arbeia would have looked.

THE RECONSTRUCTIONS

The reconstructions of the Commanding Officer's house and soldiers' quarters are strikingly different. The accommodation for the soldiers is cramped and would have been dark and uncomfortable, while the Commanding Officer's house was spacious and luxurious, with mosaics on the floors, and courtyards with fountains for him and his family to enjoy.

THE MUSEUM

Visit the museum and see the artefacts found at Arbeia which show what daily life was like for all the occupants of the fort. You will see weapons, armour and jewellery.

Discover how the Romans buried their dead and see tombstones and altars which survive to this day. These honour Romans, soldiers and civilians alike, who had come a long way from their homelands in France, Spain and Syria.

TIME QUEST

This 'hands-on' area allows visitors to dig on the excavation site and study their finds with the help of museum staff. You can piece together pottery, or try writing just as the Romans would have done.

OPENING TIMES AND GETTING THERE

1 April – 31 October:

Monday to Saturday 10 – 5.30
Sunday 1 – 5

1 November – 31 March:

Monday to Saturday 10 – 4, closed Sunday. (Closed 25 & 26 December and 1 January.)

Entry is free.

Arbeia is only a ten-minute walk from the main metro and bus station at South Shields. The fort is signposted from Ocean Road. Free car park nearby.

Website:
www.twmuseums.org.uk/arbeia

(a) How do you know from the text that Hadrian's Wall is still important today?

.... [1]

(b) Why was the situation of Arbeia Fort important to the Romans?

.... [1]

(c) How were the conditions for the officers and the ordinary soldiers different? Give **two** details for each.

Officers:

(i) ....

(ii) .... [1]

Ordinary soldiers:

(i) ....

(ii) .... [1]

(d) Name **two** things you can see in the museum that were there in Roman times.

(i) ....

(ii) .... [1]

(e) Name **three** things you can do in Time Quest.

- ....
- ....
- .... [1]

(f) What time does the Fort close in winter?

.... [1]

(g) How long does it take to walk from the bus station to Arbeia?

.... [1]

[Total: 8]

Exercise 2

In the following article, Terese Hart talks about her work in Africa for the Wildlife Conservation Society of Congo. Read the article, then answer the questions on the opposite page.

CONGO'S RARE AND BEAUTIFUL FOREST CREATURES

I spend several months a year in the Ituri rainforest in the Democratic Republic of Congo, living among the Mbuti people. My work includes studying the okapi, or forest giraffe. They are rare and beautiful creatures, with the hindquarters of a zebra, the body of an antelope and the face of their cousin, the savannah giraffe. The way they have survived for hundreds of thousands of years is to stay away from other animals, even each other. Although related to the savannah giraffe, the okapi is extremely well adapted to its forest surroundings. For example, its colours are forest colours: shadowy and dark. This is perfect camouflage, making them almost invisible at times.

As with any at-risk animal species, we have to study them if we are to save them. We need to find out where they are in the forest, what they eat and how reproductive they are. But because of their shy nature, their tendency to avoid each other, and the fact that they are spread out over a wide region, this has not been easy to do. We have found that the most successful way to study the okapi is to dig pits in the forest to catch them, with the help of Mbuti trackers. Then we attach radio collars to their necks and set them free. The radios allow us to track their activities – to know what they are doing and when they are doing it. Over the years we have built up quite a detailed picture of the way they spend their time.

When a calf is born, the female okapi hides the newborn from leopards and other animals which would prey on it and kill it. She spends a lot of the day searching for food in the forest, returning two or three times a day to nurse her calf. Pregnancy lasts a long time, around 14 months, and the young quickly learn to become independent. While a calf is dependent on its mother for food, she becomes very thin and weak.

Recent civil wars in neighbouring countries have reduced the numbers of okapi. During the wars, armies from both sides moved through the forest causing huge destruction and killing people and wildlife. There were also many refugees in the area. Another result of the conflicts was that large numbers of high-tech guns and other weapons became available, increasing the scale of hunting. Although they also hunt the okapi, the Mbuti people are traditional hunter-gatherers who live in harmony with the forest. The scale of their hunting is not destructive, as they depend on the animals and respect them.

The eco-system of the Ituri forest is very important to the welfare of the okapi. For example, two nature reserves in nearby Rwanda were cleared and made into farmland and, because the areas shared the same eco-system as the Ituri forest, the forest itself has been affected negatively. The speed at which the lovely and elusive okapi are disappearing is a big worry. We are working with other agencies, such as the World Wildlife Fund and the International Rhino Foundation. Together we approached the Congolese government and got their agreement to take action against illegal hunting and to protect the National Parks, which are vital for conservation.

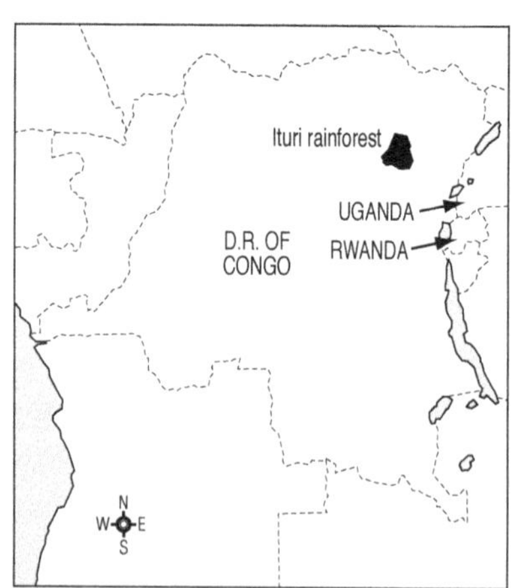

(a) Why might someone in the forest be quite close to an okapi and not be able to see it?

.... [1]

(b) Give **two** reasons why it is difficult to carry out research on the okapi.

(i) ....

(ii) .... [2]

(c) How does the research team manage to capture the okapi?

.... [1]

(d) Explain how an okapi female cares for her calf.

....

.... [2]

(e) What is the effect of the weapons that became available because of the wars?

.... [1]

(f) Why is hunting by the people who have always lived in the forest not a problem for the survival of the okapi?

.... [1]

(g) Where exactly is the Ituri rainforest?

.... [1]

(h) Describe what happened in the rainforest when neighbouring nature reserves were cleared for agriculture.

.... [1]

(i) Based on what you have read, make a list of **four** things which can be done to protect the okapi.

- ....
- ....
- ....
- .... [4]

[Total: 14]

Exercise 3

Nadia van den Brok, who came with her family from the Netherlands to live in India, attends the Bombay International College. She lives at Bungalow 4, Block 11, Kalyan Road, Bombay. Her email address is: nvandenbrok@aol.com.

Nadia's college supports the work of an international cancer research charity, Cancer Hope. This year the charity is organising a demanding three-day running competition, the Ten Hills Challenge, in the south of the country. Nadia and some of her friends decide they would like to take part.

First much fundraising must be done to cover the costs of entering the competition, and to pay for travel and accommodation. Nadia and her friends decide to do this by selling tickets for a garden party at her home, with musical entertainment. The college has offered to match what these students raise by donating an equal amount. Additionally, the students must find sponsors for the actual challenge – from among their friends, families and local businesses.

Nadia hopes that her group will all be able to stay together in a youth hostel rather than in the hotel or camping accommodation offered by the challenge organisers. Applicants must be at least 18 years old – luckily Nadia was born on 3rd July 1988. She and most of her friends are vegetarian.

College examination dates mean that the students will need to do the challenge training during the last week of January and the actual challenge during the first week of April. Nadia intends to ask her older brother to be the emergency contact during the trip. He is Ashok van den Brok and he always carries his mobile phone with him: 07703 987 765. Nadia and her fellow-students speak Dutch as their first language, but they would prefer to join an English-speaking group during the training and challenge, so that the experience will benefit their English language skills.

Imagine you are Nadia and complete the form on the opposite page, using the information above.

The Ten Hills Challenge

– raising funds for research into cancer

PARTICIPANTS' APPLICATION FORM

SECTION A

Name (in BLOCK CAPITALS): ______________________

Date of birth: ______________________

Occupation: ______________________

Country of residence: ______________________

Full address: ______________________

Email address: ______________________

Emergency contact number (family member, please): ______________________

SECTION B

Dates available for training: ______________________

Which language should the trainer use for you? (please tick)

☐ Hindi ☐ English ☐ Other (please state): ______________________

Preferred dates for actual Ten Hill Challenge (please circle):

March 30–April 1 April 4–6

Accommodation type preferred: ______________________

Please specify any special dietary requirements: ______________________

SECTION C

Write one sentence of **12–20 words** explaining how you intend to raise funds to enter the Ten Hills Challenge.

____

____

[Total: 8]

Exercise 4

Read the article below about the town of Limone in Italy which is famous for its lemons, then complete the notes on the opposite page.

Zest for Life

Does the lemon, the famous citrus fruit of Limone, contain a secret ingredient that fights heart disease? Limone, a small lemon-growing town on the shores of Lake Garda in northern Italy, holds a mystery which has made it popular with tourists in search of health. About 20 years ago scientists discovered that many people from the town (its very appropriate name means 'lemon' in Italian) had a unique protein in their blood which made them immune to heart disease. Incredibly these residents of Limone remained unaffected by heart disease even if they smoked, drank alcohol or ate large quantities of animal fat.

This discovery was wonderful for the livelihood of the people who lived in Limone; nowadays a million tourists visit their town between March and November each year. That makes 4,000 tourists per day – four times the actual population of the town. It is popularly believed that the protein must come from the lemons, which the town has grown for centuries. Until the discovery of the protein, the fruit was the only real source of income for the townspeople. Scientists have named this mysterious chemical 'apolipoprotein A1 Milano-Limone'. It is carried by 235 people, who are all descendants of a couple who married in Limone in 1644.

Lemons, which were brought to Europe from the Middle East in the 12th century, have many well-documented powers. Over the years they have been used to treat all sorts of illnesses, including typhoid, malaria, migraine and rheumatism. At its peak in the 19th century, the lemon industry in Limone produced as many as 15 million of the fruit annually. The crop was so successful because of the situation of Lake Garda: although it is relatively far north, it is shielded from the winter cold by the mountains which surround it. Also, the lemon growers here used 'limonaiae' in which to grow the lemons – rows of white stone columns linked at the top by wooden beams to form a frame that could be covered over with glass in winter or left open in warm weather. The writer D.H. Lawrence described them in his *Twilight in Italy* as 'like ruins of temples ... as if they remained from some great race that had once worshipped here'.

Nowadays, sadly, competition from southern lemon producers has meant that Limone concentrates more on its tourist industry than on lemon growing and even sells ceramic lemons as souvenirs. The few remaining growers still produce the best quality lemons, however. Signor Ezio Ceruti, a lemon producer, says, 'To grow these lemons you need to love the trees and learn from the old people who still remember how it was once done. The trees respond by being healthy and producing beautiful fruit.' Although scientists do not yet know for certain whether this fruit contains the magic ingredient that protects the people of Limone against heart disease, Signor Ceruti's recommendation for health is simple: each day slice a whole lemon into a mug, fill with boiling water, cover, leave overnight, then strain and drink.

You are going to give a short talk to your class about Limone and its lemon growing. Make **two** short notes under each heading as a basis for your talk.

THE PROTEIN FOUND IN SOME RESIDENTS' BLOOD

- .... [1]
- .... [1]

TOURISM IN LIMONE

- .... [1]
- .... [1]

GEOGRAPHICAL LOCATION

- .... [1]
- .... [1]

THE HISTORY OF LEMON GROWING

- .... [1]
- .... [1]

[Total: 8]

Exercise 5

Read the following article about the Fairtrade organisation and then write a summary describing its benefits to small farmers.

Your summary should be about 100 words. You should use your own words as far as possible.

You will be given up to 6 marks for the content of your summary, and up to 4 marks for the style and accuracy of your language.

If you think Fairtrade is just about selling coffee and tea, wake up and try our chocolate chip cookies. Why not try some Fairtrade muesli, spread a little marmalade or honey - Fairtrade of course - on your bread, and drink a glass of Fairtrade orange juice? Choose too from fresh Fairtrade bananas, mangoes, plums, oranges, pineapples, grapes and lemons. You can even choose a bunch of our hand-picked flowers.

To many of us, international trade seems an issue that does not affect us - but when world prices of cocoa or coffee beans, for example, fall it can have a devastating impact upon the lives of millions of small-scale farmers. This forces many producers into debt and many lose their land or their home and consequently their livelihood. If their means of making a living is taken away from them, they are left helpless.

Fairtrade's function is to prevent this and to ensure that all the farmers they work with get a guaranteed fair price for what they have grown, whatever the world situation. Sometimes small farmers do not even earn what it has cost them to produce their crop, but the formation of the Fairtrade certification system in the late 1980s has helped to put this situation right and has ensured a better, more stable future for thousands of producers and their families. Now many are able to build their own houses and send their children to school for the first time. Supermarkets and other retailers buy the crops direct from certified producers so that consumers can choose to buy products with the FAIRTRADE Mark, knowing they are helping the farmers who grew them.

This type of trading has brought dramatic results to the lives of some farmers. In the Dominican Republic, for example, banana producers report very positively. Since 2000 when they started selling to Fairtrade their lives have been transformed. Farmer Alfredo Martinez, who was once at the mercy of wildly changing market prices, says 'Now I have a regular income and food for my three children.' After years of living in poor-quality rented housing, farmer Gregorio Alvarez is finally building his own home since starting to sell his banana crop into the Fairtrade system.

The Fairtrade 'premium' (an additional amount paid to producers to invest in social, economic and environmental projects) has enabled Dominican farmers to provide toilets and fresh water supplies for their communities. In one area they used it to set up a community canteen where local people can get a midday meal at a reduced price. Even local sports teams have been helped with free uniforms and equipment.

Fairtrade certified products are now sold in mainstream shops in 20 countries. The range of goods is growing all the time, and so is their popularity with consumers. So look for the distinctive FAIRTRADE Mark and choose these high-quality products - not only will you enjoy them, but other people will benefit from your purchase. For more information, visit www.fairtrade.org.uk.

[10]

Exercise 6

Recently you were invited to an important family celebration held in another town. Unfortunately you were delayed on the journey and arrived late. Write a letter to a friend explaining what happened.

Your letter should be about 150–200 words long.

Don't forget to include:

- why the celebration was being held
- what kind of problem you had on the journey
- what happened in the end.

You will receive up to 9 marks for the content of your letter, and up to 9 marks for the style and accuracy of your language.

[18]

Exercise 7

Your local newspaper is leading a campaign to open a post office in your village, which will also provide internet and international telephone facilities for the community. The editor has asked people to write to the newspaper saying whether they support this idea. Here are some of the comments received:

'It's a long walk to the nearest post office at present.'

'We're looking forward to being able to buy stamps and send parcels from our own village.'

'I haven't got a computer at home and I'd like to be able to use the internet for information and communication.'

'It will cause all sorts of problems – people will crowd in to use it and drop rubbish everywhere.'

'It will create several new jobs in the village, which we really need.'

Write a letter to the newspaper giving *your* views about the idea. Your letter should be about 150–200 words long.

Begin your letter 'Dear Editor'. Do not write an address.

The comments above may give you some ideas, but you are free to use any ideas of your own.

You will receive up to 9 marks for the content of your letter, and up to 9 marks for the style and accuracy of your language.

Dear Editor,

....

....

....

....

....

....

....

....

....

....

....

....

....

....

....

....

....

....

....

....

....

....

....

.... [18]

PRACTICE TEST 2

Exercise 1

Read the following leaflet about a centre which promotes the use of alternative energy sources. Then answer the questions on the opposite page.

A unique experience awaits you at the inspirational Centre for Alternative Technology on the edge of the beautiful Snowdonia National Park.

Over thirty years ago a group of people decided to try out new, alternative technologies. They chose a remote empty quarry, where rock used to be dug from the ground, as their base. Here experiments offering solutions to the world's energy problems were carried out, and nowadays many of these ideas have become common practice. You can experience all these for yourself in just one day with us, and then take away what you have learned and put it into practice at home. Be assured it will help you save on your household energy costs!

Your visit to us begins with a ride up a steep 60-metre hillside on a railway which is worked by using the weight of water. At the summit you will enjoy stunning views to the distant coastline.

Then seven hectares of interactive displays demonstrate the power of wind, water and sun, while showing you what can be done in an ordinary household to reduce your impact on the planet.

There was no soil in the old quarry when the project was started, so we created our extensive organic gardens using our own home-made soil. You can enjoy shady woodland walks or even notice spring flowers growing on the turf roofs of environmentally-friendly buildings.

In 2006 we opened our new eco-adventure playground for children, and we also run workshops where they can make models and become inventors of the future by incorporating wind, water or solar power into their own designs.

The Centre for Alternative Technology is open all year round and has good rail, road, bus and cycle links. In fact we offer a 50% reduction on the admission price if you arrive by bicycle. There is good wheelchair access for disabled visitors — telephone us in advance if you would like assistance.

For more information, visit our website at www.cat.org.uk.

(a) Give **two** details about the location of the centre.

.... [1]

(b) What was the purpose of setting up the centre?

.... [1]

(c) How do we know that the experiments tried out at the centre were successful?

.... [1]

(d) How might a visit to the centre benefit the visitor's home?

.... [1]

(e) What sort of energy powers the railway?

.... [1]

(f) What unexpected sight awaits the visitor to the garden?

.... [1]

(g) What does the centre offer the young visitor? Name **two** things.

- ....
- .... [1]

(h) How may the visitor save money on the centre entrance fee?

.... [1]

[Total: 8]

Exercise 2

Read this article by a wildlife photographer who is interested in owls. Then answer the questions on the opposite page.

Winged silence

When I first went looking for great grey owls near my mountain home in Montana I heard their characteristic *hoo-hooing* sound long before I actually saw one. Their flight is silent, so you never know if they are nearby. Over several summers I photographed what became a familiar group of birds hunting and raising their young, as I became fascinated by their habits.

Researchers estimate that 20,000 to 100,000 great grey owls live across Canada and the USA, with similar numbers in northern Europe and Asia. They live in a range of forest habitats. Adults can weigh over 1400 grams and their wingspan is wide in relation to the weight of the bird – up to 150 cm. Their size makes it difficult for them to fly easily amongst trees. As a result, they hunt more efficiently in open spaces in forests. These spaces may have been formed by fire, wind or disease, or in many cases are man-made.

Some statistics of great grey owls

		Average for females	Average for males	Range
Length	61–84 cm	72 cm	69 cm	Both males and females can migrate many 1000s of kilometres
Wingspan	Up to 152 cm	142 cm	140 cm	
Weight	790–1454 g	1390 g	1290 g	

Great grey owls feed on small rodents like mice and voles. They have knife-sharp beaks and can locate hidden prey with the help of large facial disks which direct sounds towards their ears. They are powerful birds and dive headfirst with such force that they can crash through thick frozen snow crust to snatch small animals hidden in the deep snow beneath. They then carry their prey to a safe spot for eating before returning to the nest and their young. This hunting technique gives the great grey owls a big advantage over other birds in the same habitat.

As I photographed these birds over a period of years I began to see what marvellous and devoted parents they are. The male hunts for prey which he then delivers to the female and her chicks. She will shred the food into small pieces and drop it into their mouths. If food is scarce, the female will starve herself, losing nearly a third of her body weight in a single month, to make sure the maximum possible amount of food can go to her young chicks. The male continues to hunt by sound alone when visibility is poor, as in a snowstorm.

The chicks do not stay in the nest for more than about four weeks because, as their waste accumulates, the area around the nest develops a smell. This makes its location dangerously obvious to predators. So, even though the young owls cannot fly, they climb or fall to the ground where their parents continue to feed and protect them through the summer months. Many die of hunger or are killed, but about two-thirds survive until they are able to fly at seven to eight weeks old.

(a) How did the writer know that great grey owls were in the area he was watching?

.... [1]

(b) Why did he continue to watch them?

.... [1]

(c) What is unusual about their wings?

.... [1]

(d) Why do great grey owls hunt mainly in open spaces?

.... [1]

(e) What is the average wingspan of females?

.... [1]

(f) What is the function of the large facial disks?

.... [1]

(g) What dedication does the male great grey owl show in caring for the young?

.... [1]

(h) Describe **two** ways in which the female great grey owl cares for her young.

(i) ....

(ii) .... [2]

(i) Apart from their large facial disks, what other characteristics of the owls enable them to hunt efficiently? Give **four** details.

- ....
- ....
- ....
- .... [4]

(j) Why do the baby owls leave the nest before they can fly?

.... [1]

[Total: 14]

Exercise 3

Jamie Moran, 17, has just left school and, while he is waiting to go to university, he is working in a garage as a car washer. He lives with his twin sister Coral, and their parents Anna and Henry, at 145 Dune Street, Cork 17, in the Republic of Ireland. His email address is moranj@ecomail.com. Recently, his cousin Sophie, 24, and her baby son have moved in with the family while Sophie's husband is working abroad.

The family got an internet connection for their computer about 18 months ago, and since then they have been involved in online shopping. Jamie usually finds that when he wants to shop, everywhere is closed, so he surfs the online shopping sites. He has come across good website addresses by chance. For example, whilst researching information about a camping trip he was planning with some friends, he found a link to a website selling outdoor equipment and accessories. A special pair of binoculars was on sale, and he thought they would make a lovely birthday present for his grandfather, who loves birdwatching. The rest of the family agreed, and offered to help Jamie pay for them. To Jamie's relief, the binoculars arrived quickly, as he was worried about a possible postal delay and not having the gift in time for the birthday celebrations.

So far for himself, Jamie has bought a rare poster of a boxer he admires and a T-shirt. He was delighted with the poster, especially as only a few are in existence. The T-shirt was stylish and admired by his friends, but Coral saw a cheaper one on the local market a few days later.

Jamie's parents say he can shop online if he is careful about financial transactions. In fact, since finding some sports equipment he had been searching for without success for a long time, his father is now keen on internet shopping too.

The family haven't always been pleased with what they've bought online, however. A blue jacket Jamie's mother ordered to wear at a friend's wedding had looked wonderful, but when it arrived it was not as she had imagined. It was too tight, and the colour didn't suit her. She returned it the same day, but had to fill in a complicated form.

A website selling children's paddling pools caught Sophie's eye and she ordered one for the baby, who loves splashing in it. On checking the invoice, Sophie found she had been charged too much, but a letter of complaint to the company led to an immediate refund.

Coral prefers to handle things before she buys them, so she does not use the internet for shopping. She thinks browsing around shops with her friends and comparing prices is much more fun. As she has hardly any money, she can buy very little, but that doesn't stop her looking!

Imagine you are Jamie. Complete the following Online Shopping Evaluation Form on the opposite page on behalf of yourself and your household, using the information above.

ONLINE SHOPPING EVALUATION FORM

Section A

(Block capitals, please, for name and home address.)

Name of the person completing this form [ ]

Home address [ ]

Email address [ ]

Male / Female *(Delete)*

How many people live in your household? Adults [ ] Children under 18 [ ]

Section B

How long have you been using the internet to shop for goods or services? *(Please tick)*

0–12 months [ ] 1–2 years [ ] 2–3 years [ ] 3–5 years [ ] More than 5 years [ ]

What have been the benefits of online shopping for you or anyone in your household? *Tick any relevant statements below.*

Goods are cheaper [ ]

More convenient form of shopping [ ]

Wider range of choice for a particular product [ ]

Unusual or hard-to-find items available [ ]

Used/second-hand goods available [ ]

More anonymous way to shop [ ]

Easier to compare prices of products [ ]

Have you or anyone in your household been disappointed with online shopping services? Yes / No *(Please circle)*

If yes, please tick any relevant statements below.

Poor quality of goods [ ]

Goods not as expected [ ]

Wrong price charged [ ]

Goods arrived late [ ]

Wrong quantity supplied [ ]

Poor fit [ ]

Goods broken or damaged on arrival [ ]

Have you, or any member of your household, ever made a complaint about any goods/services bought online? Yes / No *(Please circle)*

If yes, what was the nature of the complaint? [ ]

Section C

We are interested in finding out whether online shopping is likely to replace high street shopping in the future. Write a sentence of **between 12 and 20 words** giving your opinion.

[ ]

[Total: 8]

Exercise 4

Read the article below about an unusual language, Silbo Gomero, and then complete the notes on the opposite page.

© CORBIS

SILBO GOMERO is an ancient language of whistles that enabled people to communicate across long distances ages before the invention of the telephone or the computer. It is now being revived on a volcanic island off the west coast of Africa. This is where the lovely, mountainous Canary Islands are located, and in particular the island of La Gomera. The usual language of these islands is Spanish.

The Canary Islands government is providing funding to help schoolchildren on La Gomera to learn this ancient whistling language as part of their heritage. Silbo Gomero sounds like birdsong and was developed millennia ago by islanders to enable them to communicate up to two miles across La Gomera's valleys and ravines. The Silbo language has been described as the mobile phone of the time!

In the past, Silbo Gomero had been passed down from parent to child, but the islanders felt embarrassment at such a primitive, but effective, form of communication when they came into contact with the outside world and modern technology. It started to die out when the telephone arrived and the island opened to tourism. However, the government realised what was happening and decided to make sure that children in all the island's schools learned the language so that it would not be lost. So, since 1999 Silbo Gomero has been part of the school curriculum and now about three thousand Gomeran children spend at least 25 minutes a week learning it. This is enough time for the basics to be learned.

The language probably originated in the Atlas mountains of North Africa and was brought to the island by settlers 2,500 years ago. It was adapted to Spanish speech patterns, but it uses tones rather than vowels and consonants. These are whistled at different frequencies to produce over 4,000 words, and proper conversations are possible.

'There are few really good *silbadores* (fluent whistlers of the language) so far, but lots of students are learning to use and understand Silbo Gomero. We've been very pleased with the results,' says Eugenio Darias, a Silbo teacher and director of the programme to revive the language. Really fluent *silbadores* insert a knuckle of their forefinger into their mouths, pushing the tongue back and upwards whilst using the other hand to amplify the sound.

The language's prestige is growing, and in 2003 the island held the first International Congress of Whistled Languages. Research is now being carried out in Venezuela, Cuba and Texas, all places to which Gomerans have traditionally emigrated and where forms of the language survive. The Canary government's Historical Heritage Department believes that Silbo is the most important pre-Hispanic cultural heritage the islands have and are hoping to attract outside support so that it will continue.

You are going to give a short talk to explain Silbo Gomero to your class. Make short notes under each heading as a basis for your talk.

Origins and purpose of Silbo Gomero

- .... [1]
- .... [1]

Features of the language

- .... [1]
- .... [1]
- .... [1]

Why the language was disappearing

- .... [1]

How the language is being revived

- .... [1]
- .... [1]

[Total: 8]

Exercise 5

Read the following article about Baldev Singh, who became a teacher at the age of 39. Write a summary about how this changed his life and the lives of his pupils.

You should write about 100 words, and you should use our own words as far as possible.

You will be given up to 6 marks for the content of your summary, and up to 4 marks for the style and accuracy of your language.

The IT specialist whose pupils all work together... in India and Bristol

Some people thought Baldev Singh was mad when he gave up his well-paying job as a university researcher to teach biology to twelve-year-olds. 'I used to have to do some teaching to medical students at the university,' he says, 'and I realised it was the part of the job I enjoyed most.' He decided he liked working with people rather than being on his own in a laboratory. So, at the age of 39, he became a newly-qualified teacher of biology at a school of 1,100 pupils in Bristol, England, which specialises in science and technology.

Six years later, his job has taken him to Cairo, Jordan and Johannesburg. He managed this because of his desire to bring difficult subjects to life by using computers and IT. He moved away from just teaching biology and introduced a citizenship course called 'eCitizenship' using information technology. This motivated the children better than anything else he could have thought of because it allowed them to use and develop their skills in a more meaningful and practical way. Baldev says that asking pupils to produce, for example, a chart showing different types of drinks served in the school canteen was boring, but asking them to analyse census data for Bristol and produce a bar chart of the diverse communities in which they live was much more motivating for them.

Building on this idea and using a piece of software called 'Gemini', Baldev linked his school in the UK with a school in India. Using the internet, the pupils of both schools were able to communicate and collaborate on a project in which they explored why there is conflict in certain parts of the world. It offered them the chance to ask and answer questions about their daily lives using an internet chatroom facility.

A second project was soon started in South Africa, and again pupils exchanged information about themselves, their hobbies, families and schools. Baldev even went to South Africa in his summer holidays to help train police cadets to run citizenship workshops. He was invited to Cairo to help on a training scheme for new IT teachers there, and in Jordan he was part of a group looking at the new Information Technology curriculum for schools.

All this was because of the excellent research skills which he brought with him to school teaching from his previous job in university research. He constantly experiments with the effects of new technology on education and training.

Baldev no longer teaches biology and is now Head of his school's IT department. He is still full of enthusiasm, and he says that what he does in school doesn't feel like work at all. He is excited by the idea that his pupils' learning now goes a long way beyond the actual classroom walls. As information technology is changing and developing so fast, he says that the pupils sometimes know more than their teachers. He sees himself less as a teacher than as a gatekeeper to the wide world of information.

[10]

Exercise 6

> **Is your teacher special?**
>
> **Tell us why he or she deserves to win this year's**
>
> **OUTSTANDING TEACHER AWARD**
>
> **Your letter should reach us by 30th June.**

You have seen this notice in your local college and decide to write a letter to the college Principal nominating one of your teachers.

Your letter should be about 150–200 words long.

Don't forget to explain:

- who the award should go to
- why the award should be given
- what is special about the named teacher.

You will receive up to 9 marks for the content of your letter, and up to 9 marks for the style and accuracy of your language.

[18]

Exercise 7

The members of your college History Society believe that history should not be seen as just a list of dates and events but as an important part of our daily lives. To make people aware of the importance of history they are organising a campaign called 'History Matters'.

Here are some of the comments they have received from people they have talked to:

'Buildings, paintings, institutions, landscapes and horizons are all part of our history.'

'People matter, not history.'

'History is all about the past; we need to worry about the present.'

'We need to understand history to understand what is happening now.'

'Each day we write our own history.'

Write an article for your college magazine giving *your* views on the subject. Your article should be about 150–200 words long.

The comments above may give you some ideas, but you are free to use any ideas of your own.

You will receive up to 9 marks for the content of your article, and up to 9 marks for the style and accuracy of your language.

[18]

PRACTICE TEST 3

Exercise 1

Read the following advice leaflet about food labels and then answer the questions on the opposite page.

What's on your food label?

Nowadays we all know that it's best to eat healthily, limiting our intake of fat, sugar and salt. We at Fineways Supermarkets have reduced the levels of these in 1000 of our products and are doing so for a further 950 this year. In addition, we have introduced a new labelling system to help you make informed choices as you purchase food, in order to maintain a healthy diet and way of life.

When you buy food, you the consumer need to know exactly what you will be eating. Some products are already labelled 'Healthy' or 'Low in fat', but don't rely on that; we would rather the customer decides after reading the nutritional information on the packet. So our new food labels have become

clearer and more helpful, providing an at-a-glance breakdown of the nutritional value of each product.

Our easy-to-read labels explain simply what is in your food. They show you:

- how much sugar, fat and salt are in each serving
- how many calories one serving contains
- the percentages of your guideline daily amounts (GDAs) for each of these.

What are Guideline Daily Amounts?

GDAs are a guide to the total amount of calories, sugar, fat, salt and other elements we should eat in a day. According to experts, GDAs for a typical adult are:

Calories	2000 kcal
Sugar	90 g
Fat	70 g
Salt	6 g

Please note that children and active adults have different nutritional requirements. For more information visit www.foodlabels.com/health.

Numbers count

Here is an example of our new labelling:

Chicken salad sandwich pack		
Calories	256	13% GDA
Sugar	3.1 g	4% GDA
Fat	4.8 g	7% GDA
Salt	1.1 g	19% GDA

Knowing this kind of information about each product you buy means that you can mix healthy foods with less healthy treats, while still keeping within the recommended daily amounts.

So be informed about your shopping with Fineways' easy new health-conscious labels!

(a) According to the text, what should be restricted in a good diet?

.... [1]

(b) What has already been done, and what is currently happening, to help Fineways' customers to eat more healthily? Give **two** details.

(i) ....

(ii) .... [1]

(c) How are the Fineways new food labels more helpful than they used to be?

.... [1]

(d) How does the reader know that the new labelling system is not difficult?

.... [1]

(e) Apart from actual contents, what else do the new food labels show?

.... [1]

(f) How exactly can the consumer find out more about the recommended daily amounts?

.... [1]

(g) What percentage of the recommended daily amount of salt does the chicken salad sandwich contain?

.... [1]

(h) Describe a practical advantage for the shopper of the new labelling system.

.... [1]

[Total: 8]

Exercise 2

Read the following article and then answer the questions on the opposite page.

EDUCATING CHILDREN THROUGH SPORT

What has educating children through sport got to do with health? In fact it has everything to do with the future health of the next generation, both physically and mentally. Several countries have therefore introduced an 'education through sport' project in a number of schools across Europe.

The focus for the children is a variety of sports-related activities, including drawing and design using computers and conventional materials, as well as taking part in actual games and sports events. This is to raise their awareness of sport and to counteract modern European children's increasing tendency to sit and watch television or play computer games in their free time, whilst snacking on junk foods. Governments see the project as a valuable way of halting the increase in obesity and related diseases in the young.

The organisers felt that a good way to educate children about sport was to start with the Olympic Games. In this way they can learn about and discuss a whole range of sports and how they started. Books have been specially produced to help with this, and each book is age-specific so that it can explain the Games clearly in language the children will understand for their age group. Events like the Marathon and the Pentathlon are explained, as well as more familiar sports such as rowing, horse riding and tennis. Children will also look at the Paralympic Games for disabled athletes. They can talk via the internet to competitors like Cathy Mitton, who is a wheelchair user and Paralympic table tennis player. She encourages other disabled athletes to compete and enjoy their sport, whatever it is, and comments that one great advantage for her is the opportunity to travel.

Educating children through sport can also be useful in highlighting cultural differences. For example, some countries concentrate on only a few sports such as football or volleyball, with the result that the children of those countries remain ignorant of the huge selection of sports available. Some countries have sports that are weather-specific and nationally supported, like waterpolo and sailing in Malta, whereas skiing and cricket are not practised so much there as they are in, say, Austria or the UK.

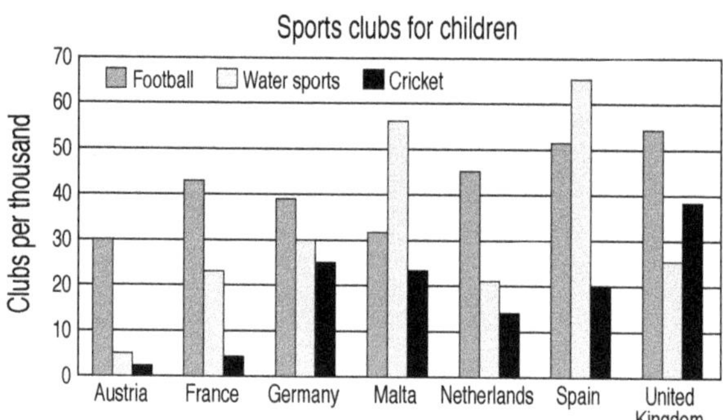

The organisers of the project hope, not only to improve the fitness of children throughout Europe, but also to develop important aspects of sport such as fair play, respect for others, teamwork, the desire to win, and many other values which seem to be disappearing from today's society. It is hoped that all the work on this project will lead to more confident children who can handle stress much better in the future and remain healthy into adulthood. In addition, the social advantages are increased self-respect, and confidence in their own ability to compete and win in things other than sport.

Finally, educating children through sport has no boundaries – young, old and those with special needs can all take part.

(a) What is the main aim of 'education through sport'?

.... [1]

(b) As well as taking part in games and sports events, what else are children expected to do and use on the project? Give **two** things.

.... [1]

(c) Why are governments in Europe supporting this project?

.... [1]

(d) How can books on the Olympic Games help all children on the project?

.... [1]

(e) What is unusual about the sportsperson Cathy Mitton?

.... [1]

(f) What does she particularly enjoy about taking part in the Paralympics?

.... [1]

(g) What is the disadvantage to children in countries where only one or two sports are practised?

.... [1]

(h) Why are water polo and sailing popular in Malta?

.... [1]

(i) Which country on the chart has the most water sports clubs for children?

.... [1]

(j) Which sport seems to be popular in all the countries on the chart?

.... [1]

(k) What qualities will be developed in children who take part in the project? Name **four** things.

- ....
- ....
- ....
- ....[4]

[Total: 14]

Exercise 3

Simon and Hazel Tomas, parents of 16-year-old Andrea, are encouraging their daughter to compete for an award which would provide funds for her private music lessons for the next three years.

The 'Musical Excellence Award' pays for an hourly lesson each week for thirty weeks of the year, with the music teacher of the candidate's choice. Andrea's main instrument is the clarinet, and she has always learned with Mrs Schmidt and would not wish to change teachers at this stage. With the clarinet Andrea has recently reached the Performance Diploma stage, having successfully completed her Grade 8 examination two years ago. She plays for the Regional Junior Orchestra and leads the clarinet section – there are four other players under her guidance in this orchestra. She also plays the piano and is awaiting the results of her Grade 7 examination which she took three weeks ago. She enjoys singing, has a lovely soprano voice and is a member of two choirs, each of which has weekly practices. One of the choir directors, Mr Braun, will write her a reference for the 'Musical Excellence Award' application, and Andrea has already asked Mrs Schmidt to write her a testimonial letter saying how long she has known her and confirming the standard of her playing.

Andrea has to send in an application form in order to obtain an audition for the award. She is rather worried about practising and playing two contrasting pieces successfully to the award judges because of her heavy IGCSE examination schedule during the audition period of 4th – 8th June; in fact she can only attend on Wednesday 6th or Thursday 7th June. She has to be available to be contacted by the award committee and luckily she has her own mobile phone, 07779 683259, and her own email address, atomas@yahoo.com. She must provide bank details in case she is successful in achieving an award. Her bank identification code is 42-70-11 and her account number is 93537352.

Andrea also has to confirm that she can attend the spring residential course next year, which is compulsory for all award holders and is a condition of taking up the award. This should not be a problem for her, as her school has agreed to allow her to attend even if the course is during term time.

Andrea hopes to study music at university and then to follow a postgraduate course leading to becoming a conductor, or a director of an orchestra.

Imagine you are Andrea. Complete the application form on the opposite page, using the information above.

APPLICATION FORM: MUSICAL EXCELLENCE AWARD

SECTION A: CONTACT DETAILS

Name: ______________________________ Age: ______________

Telephone: ______________________ E-mail: ______________________

Bank code: ______________________ Account number: ______________________

Availability during award audition period: 4th 5th 6th 7th 8th June *(please circle as many days as possible)*

For applicants under 18 years, please supply names of parents/guardians:

____

SECTION B: RELEVANT MUSICAL EXPERIENCE

Main instrument: ______________________________

Level of achievement: ______________________________

Other musical instruments/abilities: ______________________________

Positions of responsibility held: ______________________________

____

SECTION C: FURTHER DETAILS

If successful in obtaining an award, I wish to learn with :

______________________________ *(supply name of preferred teacher)*

I confirm that I am able to attend next year's spring residential course, from 6 – 12 April:

YES NO *(delete as necessary)*

Names and status of two referees:

1) Name: ______________________ Status: ______________________

2) Name: ______________________ Status: ______________________

SECTION D

In the space below, write **one sentence of between 12 and 20 words** giving details of any relevant future plans.

____

____

[Total: 8]

Exercise 4

Read the article below about the ancient Babylonians, then complete the notes on the opposite page.

THE BABYLONIANS

The remains of the city of Babylon are now in Iraq, about 150 kilometres south of present-day Baghdad. The city was at one time the splendid capital of an empire. Its position on the banks of the River Euphrates, which has a fertile flood plain, made it rich in agricultural produce. These crops were traded with foreign nations for precious metals and stones, and for ivory, silk and wood. Manufactured goods (mainly textiles) were another important part of the economy.

The Babylonian empire was at its greatest in about 600 BC, when it stretched from the coast of the Mediterranean in the west to the border of Persia in the east; and from the River Tigris in the north to the Arabian desert in the south.

We know a good deal about this empire and its well-developed civilization and culture. This is because the Babylonian language, known as Akkadian, has survived in written form. The writing system, known as cuneiform, was made up of triangle-like marks cut in pieces of clay or stone, many of which have been found. After much hard work by scholars in the nineteenth century, Akkadian can now be understood and translated. The result is that, as well as examples of Babylonian literature, we have written evidence of what went on in everyday society.

There are, for example, records of government and business activities, from which we know that the Babylonians invented a system of weights and measures which was later used by the Greeks and Romans. Many metal or stone weights, often in the shape of ducks, have been found and can now be seen in museums. We know, too, of the Babylonians' excellence in the field of mathematics – a large number of texts involving geometry and algebra of a quite sophisticated sort have been preserved. Surgery was known, and even delicate eye operations were performed.

Astronomy and astrology were studied, as they were closely connected to the Babylonian religion, which played an extremely important role in society. Each city had its own chief god or goddess who was worshipped at his or her special temple. The god of the city of Babylon, for example, was Bel, or Marduk, who was the king of the gods, the equivalent of the Greek god Zeus. There were elaborate daily rituals involving the presentation of food offerings to the gods in their temples and the cleaning of their garments.

The Babylonian empire was ruled by a king, who had absolute power. The most famous was Nebuchadnezzar II. The basic units of society were the tribe and the family. An individual's social class was determined by that of his family, and a Babylonian without a family was a rare and miserable creature. For this reason, adoption was very common. Urban communities were an important feature of Babylonian civilization, and the plain was dotted with cities, notably Babylon, Sippar, Kish, Nippur and Ur.

You are preparing to give a short talk to your class about the Babylonians. Make short notes under each heading as a basis for your talk.

BABYLONIAN ECONOMY BASED ON

- .... [1]
- .... [1]

LANGUAGE

- .... [1]
- .... [1]

SCIENTIFIC ACHIEVEMENTS

- .... [1]
- .... [1]

RELIGION IN BABYLONIAN SOCIETY

- *extremely important*
- .... [1]

SOCIAL ORGANISATION

- .... [1]
- *tribe and family*
- *many cities*

[Total: 8]

Exercise 5

Read the following article about students studying in India. Write a summary describing why they are so keen to go the Indian Institute of Technology and what they need to do to prepare.

You should write about 100 words, and you should use your own words as far as possible.

You will be given up to 6 marks for the content of your summary, and up to 4 marks for the style and accuracy of your language.

In a class of their own

In Patna, in eastern India, the 500 students at the Ramanujan Mathematical Academy are so keen to learn that they will put up with overcrowding, even standing for hours in the horribly high temperatures, just to hear their lectures and get a chance to study. This is because they want to get to the elite Indian Institute of Technology, a network of seven universities known collectively as IITs.

In terms of technology, the IITs are shaping not only India but the world, so it is no wonder that students are so keen to graduate from them. Some of the most successful graduates include the head of Vodaphone and the inventor of Hotmail.

To achieve this level of fame and success, or just a very good degree from an IIT, students must first go to a small educational academy like the Ramanujan Academy. Every student in the class dreams of getting into an IIT, even though only 40 out of 200,000 applicants a year are successful in entering this prestigious world of learning. The Ramanujan students are eager to impress – when the teacher asks a question, a hundred hands shoot up into the air. Most of the students are from extremely poor villages in the district and they know that thirty of them will be selected by the academy for special intensive coaching. The so-called Super 30 pay no fees and are also given basic accommodation, so competition is fierce.

Once they have managed to complete the course at the academy, students have to take two three-hour exams and be in the top two per cent to gain a place at an IIT. If they fail, they simply have to try again. To get the high grades required, many students study for up to sixteen hours a day, and even that does not guarantee that they will get onto the exact university course they want.

The parents of many of the students are uneducated farmers who do not always understand what their children want to be or do. However, this does not stop the students from having high ambitions. For example, Krishna Rai aged 19 wants to do aerospace engineering and one day travel and work in space. He believes that technology will transform the world and allow people to live on other planets in the future. He feels this is vital as the earth is becoming overcrowded. His father, Gopal Rai, would prefer him to get a good job in India and buy some land in his home village.

All the students attending the academy have an unshakeable optimism that they will succeed, and they firmly believe that studying technology will enable them to live a more comfortable and easier life than their parents have done. It is vital that they get the IIT place they dream of, because failure for them is not an option.

.... [10]

Exercise 6

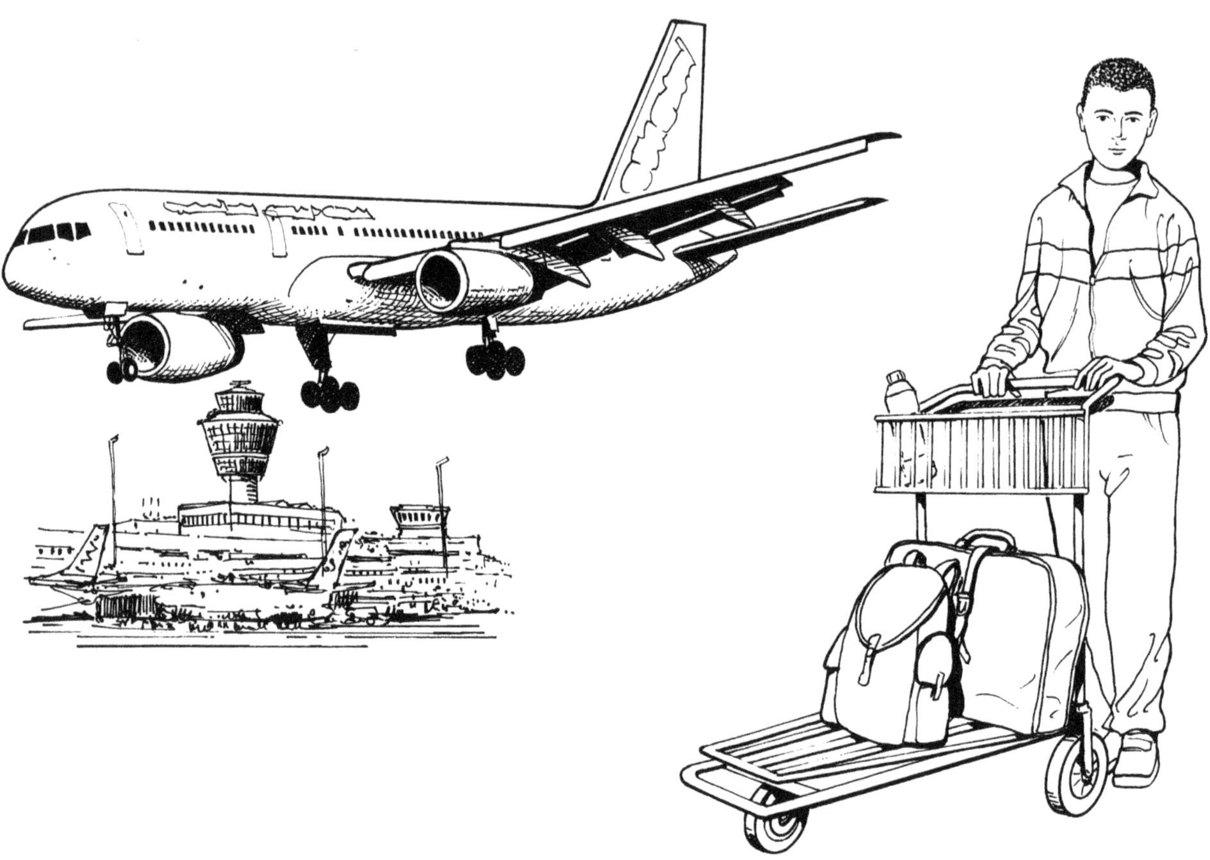

A foreign friend is coming to stay with you and your family for a short visit. You decide to write a letter explaining:

- what they can look forward to doing with you and your family
- what they will need to bring with them
- things they will find different from their own country.

Your letter should be about 150–200 words long.

You will receive up to 9 marks for the content of your letter, and up to 9 marks for the style and accuracy of your language.

[18]

Exercise 7

Experts have discovered that some people are not getting enough folic acid, a vitamin important for health, in their diet. They are suggesting that folic acid (which is found naturally in some green vegetables) should be added artificially to bread. Here are some comments from people you have discussed this with:

'I don't mind as long as the bread doesn't cost more or taste any different.'

'No way! I like my bread just as it is. Experts don't have the right to interfere with how I eat!'

'Good idea! It'll make us healthier, and I think we'd rather get folic acid from bread than from vegetables.'

'I'm against it! We could get too much of this vitamin, or be unable to absorb it from bread. We could end up being less healthy.'

Write a letter to your local newspaper giving *your* views on the suggestion.
Your letter should be about 150–200 words long.

Begin your letter 'Dear Editor'. Do not write an address.

The comments above may give you some ideas, but you are free to use any ideas of your own.

You will receive up to 9 marks for the content of your letter, and up to 9 marks for the style and accuracy of your language.

Dear Editor,

....

....

....

....

....

....

....

....

....

....

....

....

....

....

....

....

....

....

....

....

....

....

....

.... [18]

PRACTICE TEST 4

Exercise 1

Read the following information about a science museum and then answer the questions on the opposite page.

Would you like to build and launch your own rocket? Do you like inventing your own gadgets? Do you want to find out how things work?

If so, come and visit our 5 floors of interactive exhibits. Find out about the weather, aeroplanes and ships, or discover how the computer developed. There's something for the whole family – the youngest can push brightly-lit buttons and watch how things work, while grandparents can enjoy our classic cars and planes.

Why not visit our two current temporary exhibitions? The first, **Dead Ringers**, shows how the mobile phone has created a huge global waste problem. Up to 50 million are thrown away each year; we show how scientists and charities are working together to combat this and how you can help. In our **50 Years of Cartoon** exhibition, you can come behind the scenes with us and see how your favourite animated characters were created.

Then really become part of the action in our **3D Cinema**. Only 12 people have ever walked on the Moon's surface and now you can be the next – you will even feel the Moon dust flying into your face! Or take part in our cinema's 3D wildlife adventure. You will search for and see elephant, rhino, buffalo, lion and leopard, closely but safely.

Now stop to buy a snack in our award-winning **Deep Water Café** or use any of the special picnic areas. Finally stop at our **shop** on the way out – here you will find everything you need to carry out your own experiments, along with books and educational games.

Opening hours are 10 – 6 daily and entrance is free. Visit our website at www.sciencemuseum.org for updates on events. *Please note: some displays use flashing lights. No photography or video-recording are permitted inside the museum.*

(a) How do you know the museum is suitable for all ages?

.... [1]

(b) How can small children learn from a visit to the museum?

.... [1]

(c) What are the purposes of the exhibitions which are in the museum for only a short time?

(i) ....

(ii) .... [2]

(d) What can visitors experience in the 3D Cinema? Give **two** details.

(i) ....

(ii) .... [1]

(e) Why can the Deep Water Café be recommended?

.... [1]

(f) How can you be really up to date with the events in the museum?

.... [1]

(g) What health and safety warning is given by the museum?

.... [1]

[Total: 8]

Exercise 2

Read this article carefully and then answer the questions on the opposite page.

EDEN: A LIVING THEATRE OF PLANTS, PEOPLE AND POSSIBILITIES

A giant seed, the largest stone sculpture in the world, has become the new symbol of the Eden Project. This 70-tonne work of art symbolises Eden's purpose – to be a place where plants and ideas can grow.

The newly-arrived Seed

Height:	4 metres
Width:	3 metres
Weight:	70 tonnes (cut from 167-tonne piece of rock)
Material:	granite, one of Earth's toughest rocks
Completed:	2007

The Eden Project opened in Cornwall in the south-west of England in 2001 and was immediately hailed as the Eighth Wonder of the World. This regeneration project has transformed some empty, abandoned clay pits into fertile, living land housing a tropical rainforest, a botanical garden and a constantly changing, living theatre of plants and people. Its aim is to be 'a place for current thinking about future possibilities for the environment'.

Eden has already attracted more than 10 million visitors to the distinctive domes or 'biomes' which have been its trademark symbol until now. The first, the Humid Tropics Biome, houses the sights, sounds, smells and scale of the endangered rainforest landscape. Tropical plants are grown here; their use in everyday products such as medicines, food and beauty preparations, and their management for the future are carefully explained. The daily life of the rainforest regions is reconstructed by means of buildings, webcams, video recordings and even geographical features such as waterfalls – all under the dome. The world's largest and smelliest flower, the Titan arum (or 'corpse flower') from Sumatra, has recently bloomed here – it flowers only once, for 48 hours, and then dies. So many rare and significant experiences and events are offered at Eden, and all are so easily accessible for the visitor.

The same approach to educating the visitor about the global environment is taken in the second dome-shaped conservatory. Here the sweet scents of olive, orange and lemon trees mingle with herbs, a recreation of Mediterranean, Southern African and Californian fragrances.

Perhaps surprisingly, 75 per cent of Eden's plants are grown outside. There are terraces of plants which have changed the world – hemp, lavender and tea, for example. The Eden Project is the only place in the world where cocoa beans grow across the path from sunflowers, and where a field of poppies looks down on tea and rice plantations further down the gentle, sunny slope.

There is a sunflower-shaped education centre to help visitors from all over the world. Called 'the Core', it is listed as one of the top ten buildings in the UK for using renewable energy. The giant seed sculpture has been 'planted' here in the heart of Eden, the biggest piece of rock art moved since the Egyptians showed us how. It symbolises the idea that education and awareness can lead the way in helping to stabilise the future of the world's environment.

(a) Why is the giant sculpture shaped like a seed?

.... [1]

(b) What material was used for the sculpture and why is this special?

.... [1]

(c) What was the original weight of the rock?

.... [1]

(d) What was the Eden Project known by before the seed sculpture arrived?

.... [1]

(e) Apart from the plants, how can the visitor experience life in a rainforest in the first dome? Give **two** examples.

(i) ....

(ii) .... [2]

(f) What is significant about the blooming of the special flower?

.... [1]

(g) What is the function of the outside display?

.... [1]

(h) How can the reader measure the success of Eden so far? Give **one** detail from the article.

.... [2]

(i) Give **four** examples of how the Eden Project is helping the environment.

- ....
- ....
- ....
- .... [4]

[Total: 14]

Exercise 3

GREETINGS is an organisation which places students in voluntary holiday work worldwide. Volunteers work as tour guides at historic sites and monuments, and in historic buildings such as castles, mansions and palaces. They volunteer for one month at a time to greet, welcome and guide visitors. Applicants are offered some choice of location for their placement, and a working knowledge of the local language is essential. In addition to guiding tourists and visitors, applicants must be prepared to help on information desks and in the shops within the historic places. They must make and pay for their own return travel arrangements, but free accommodation and food are provided.

Applicants for a GREETINGS placement must be reliable and able to get on easily with people. Two references are required, one of which must be from the Head of the applicant's place of study. A compulsory training weekend is held centrally in the home country of each applicant, and this includes teamwork, practice tours and giving presentations.

Shiraz Malawi is nearly 18 and lives in Sri Lanka at 3500 Puttalam Avenue, Colombo. He is just finishing his studies at Sri Lanka Main School (Head: Mr A Malik). He wishes to spend a month after he leaves school doing voluntary work, preferably in southern Europe. He is available in July and early August, before he joins his father for a visit to his uncle in America in August/September. He has studied French and Spanish to GCSE level, as well as A-level History, English, Italian and Fine Art (his chosen university subject).

Shiraz thinks that working for GREETINGS will enable him to help others while giving him some work experience and the opportunity to practise his language skills. Eventually he wants to work in the conservation of old buildings. His current experience is his weekend voluntary work at the Local History Museum in Sea Road, Colombo, where Mr B Premadasa is curator and would certainly recommend him for the position of volunteer guide.

Shiraz's email address is smalawi@yahoo.com and his telephone number is 0094-216-6790925.

Imagine you are Shiraz. Fill in the application form on the opposite page, applying for a one-month placement with GREETINGS, using the information above.

GREETINGS INTERNATIONAL VOLUNTEER GROUP

Tour guide application form

(Please write your name and address in CAPITALS.)

PART A

Name: ....

Age: .... Male / Female (*please delete*)

Address: ....

....

Telephone number: ....

Email address: ....

PART B

Name of school or college: ....

Languages studied and level of proficiency: ....

....

PART C

Preferred placement location (*please circle one*):

Africa Americas Asia Australasia Europe

Available month (*please circle one*):

May June July August September January February

PART D

Please provide details of 2 relevant referees:

1) Name: ....

Institution and position held:

....

2) Name: ....

Institution and position held:

....

PART E

Please write one sentence of **12–20 words** explaining why you feel you are a suitable candidate to be a GREETINGS volunteer.

....

....

[Total: 8]

Exercise 4

Read the article below about Oymyakon, a village in Russia, and then complete the notes on the opposite page.

FROZEN IN TIME

The temperature is below minus 30 as the children skip through the icy snow without their hats. Their fathers and older brothers who are working outside – chopping ice, splitting wood and carrying cubes of frozen milk home to their families – have stripped off their warm outer layers. 'Oh, it's very warm,' says Lyudmila Repina, a teacher, as she begins a Russian class for 10-year-olds. 'We think minus 40 at this time of year is good, but minus 30 is amazing. Today the children will be playing outside during breaktime.'

The Russian village of Oymyakon, in far north-eastern Siberia, is one of the coldest places on earth and winter temperatures can fall into the minus sixties. The village is more than 200 miles south of the Arctic Circle but about 6000 feet up in the Verkhoyansk mountains, which is what makes it so cold. For thousands of years the region was home only to nomads who lived off reindeer herds. Today it is one of Russia's richest regions, with some of the world's largest gold and diamond deposits. Even so, like their ancestors, locals still keep a gun in the house and hunt and fish to bring food to the family table.

© Dean Conger/CORBIS

Despite the severity of the winter, people say they love the climate and look forward to the winter. Valentin, a local, says 'The cold keeps you healthy and kills bacteria. People here are very special. It's probably because the conditions are so difficult it forces us to work together. Life here might seem difficult to you, but we have clean air, clean food, mushrooms and berries. I could live in Moscow, but here is where I want to be. It's the land of hunting and fishing. We are happy.' During the short but hot summer people work from daybreak until sunset in the fields. 'The summer is very hard work,' says Marianna, a 35-year-old teacher at the school. 'We have three cows and we have to cut grass for them all day, to feed them through the long winter.'

With a population of about 1,000, Oymyakon has a small hospital, a spacious school and a shop selling imported sweets and biscuits. Municipal buildings are heated by huge insulated pipes that snake across the snowy landscape. Many villagers have computers and, although mobile phones don't work here, they have direct telephone lines.

Wood rather than stone is used to build houses, as it is more flexible and lighter. Because of the sub-zero temperatures there is no plumbing, so the lavatory is an outhouse with a small hole in the floor, usually some distance from the house. Water for cooking is kept outside in blocks of ice that are brought into the warm house to be melted before use. Fish and meat are kept in a storage room under the house which can be reached from inside the kitchen.

You are preparing to give a short talk to your class about winter in Oymyakon. Make short notes for your talk under each heading.

Location of the village of Oymyakon

- .... [1]
- .... [1]

How homes are adapted to the climate

- .... [1]
- .... [1]
- .... [1]

Traditional diet

- .... [1]
- .... [1]
- .... [1]

[Total: 8]

Exercise 5

Read the following article about bats. Then write a summary about their physical characteristics and behaviour, and how declining bat populations can be helped.

You should write about 100 words. You should use your own words as far as possible.

You will receive up to 6 marks for the content of your summary, and up to 4 marks for the style and accuracy of your language.

THE WORLD OF BATS

There are 1,100 species of bats worldwide, making up about 20 per cent of all mammal species. Bats are the only mammals capable of flying long distances and are sometimes called 'flying mice'. These interesting animals are classified by scientists as the Order *Chioptera*, which means 'hand-wing' in Greek, and the name highlights the similarity of a bat's wing to an outspread human hand. Bats are as small as a plum and the weight of only ten paperclips!

Two-thirds of all bats are insect-eaters, each consuming thousands of insects in one night. Other bats eat fruit, apart from three blood-eating species, several types which feed on fish, and the spectral bat and ghost bat of Australia which even prey on other bats. Bats' teeth are sharp in order to bite through insect armour or fruit skin.

Most bats chase their prey from dusk until dawn, using high-pitched sounds to locate insects. They listen and then swoop, seizing the insects with their feet. They can hunt in complete darkness using these echo-location calls; the echoes (also used by dolphins and whales) produce a sound picture of their immediate surroundings. Young children can often hear bats calling, as their ears are sensitive to such sound levels.

Bats need our help as some species are now endangered. The mouse-eared bat was even thought to be extinct until one was recently discovered hanging upside down in an old railway tunnel. A mother bat produces only one baby bat or 'pup' each year, and this is not enough to maintain bat populations where predators (mainly owls), spoiled habitat and sensitivity to climate change all lower the rate of survival.

Climate change, however, could also affect bat populations positively, since warmer weather encourages insect populations and therefore bats. To encourage bats, scented night plants, such as honeysuckle, which attract insects can be planted. Trees are useful sources of food and roosting sites, and the provision of ponds is another possible way of encouraging insects for bat food. Bat roosting boxes can be made from wood and positioned on trees, walls or even in city gardens.

Bats are now protected by law – if a colony is denied its roosting site because of preservation work on an old house, for example, then an alternative site for the bats must be provided. Protection groups now monitor bat behaviour and habitat, and bat sightings are reported by volunteers to help accumulate information. These protection groups produce leaflets about bat boxes and bat care, designed to promote public awareness, and there are night-time bat walks and bat watches using ultrasound detectors. Bat Conservation Trust visitors can even watch colonies of bats in an attic or under the eaves of a roof using a 'Bat Cam' web camera. Visit their website at www.bats.org to find out more.

[10]

Exercise 6

How do you feel about being the age you are now?

Is being a teenager the best or worst age to be?

Write to us with your views and we'll pay $10 for every article we print and $15 for the Star article!

You have just seen this announcement in *Magical*, a teenage magazine.

Write an article for the magazine giving your views. Your article should be about 150–200 words long.

In your article you should:

- say how old you are and what you enjoy about being the age you are now
- explain what teenagers can find difficult about teenage life
- say what you think the best age to be is.

You will receive up to 9 marks for the content of your article, and up to 9 marks for the style and accuracy of your language.

[18]

Exercise 7

Your local museum has invited the public to make suggestions about improving the facilities for students and other visitors. Here are some ideas from local people:

'It would be interesting to know more about the things in the museum but the labels aren't very clear.'

'We need somewhere to sit down after looking round.'

'I'd like to be able to touch the exhibits to see what they are really like.'

'The buses only go past the end of the road, which isn't very convenient.'

Write a letter to the Director of the museum giving *your* suggestions.
Your letter should be about 150–200 words long.

Begin your letter 'Dear Director'. Do not write an address.

The comments above may give you some ideas, but you are free to use any ideas of your own.

You will receive up to 9 marks for the content of your letter, and up to 9 marks for the style and accuracy of your language.

Dear Director,

....

....

....

....

....

....

....

....

....

....

....

....

....

....

....

....

....

....

....

....

....

....

....

.... [18]

KEY

Marking the language aspect of the summary

Use the table below as a guide to help you focus on specific elements when marking the fluency, cohesion and clarity of the students' answers. Award marks according to the table.

4 marks The student has excellent language skills and resources and is able to write a coherent, sustained summary, mainly in his/her own words. He/she shows analytical skills in interpreting the task. The writing flows well, with smooth linking between ideas. These are expressed concisely and there is a strong sense of summary style. The summary is close to the word limit, and may be divided into more than one paragraph if appropriate (Extended candidates only). Ambitious vocabulary, however, or elaborate sentence constructions are not necessary for full marks.	**1 mark** The student's writing shows some understanding of the text and the question set, but overall the writing is too general and shows little sense of an appropriate summary style. The standard of language is weak. There may be mistakes in basic construction, punctuation or spelling so that occasionally the meaning is unclear. There are few or no connectors and/or they may be used incorrectly. This gives the writing a rambling effect. There may be a tendency to write a simple list of items or to copy a substantial amount from the text. Some of the material in the summary may be unconnected to the question. This may include ideas not given in the text, and the student's own opinions. There is no attempt to keep to the word limit.
3 marks The student shows a good understanding of the text and the task set, and writes with a high degree of organisation and control. Sentences are usually straightforward and accurate, and the meaning is clear. There is little misspelling. Some connectors are used to link ideas and to help make the summary coherent and orderly. The student has sufficient language resources and breadth of vocabulary to put ideas from the text into his/her own words quite often.	**0 marks** The content of what the student has written is completely irrelevant and shows no understanding of the text or the question set. His/her language errors are so numerous as to make communication incomprehensible.
2 marks The student makes some attempt to respond accurately to the task and to develop a clear, organised summary using some connectors. There may, however, be lapses where pieces are copied from the original text, and some of the copying may contain irrelevance. Basic punctuation, such as capitals and full stops, is accurate, and simple words are spelled accurately. Sentence construction is generally satisfactory, but limited language resources and response to the task may produce, overall, a fragmented effect.	

Marking exercises 6 and 7

Note: At Core level, up to 5 marks are available for content and up to 5 marks for language. At Extended level, up to 9 marks are available for each.

Marks	CONTENT: Relevance and development of ideas	Marks	LANGUAGE: Style and accuracy
8–9	**Highly effective** ***Relevance:*** Fulfils the task, with consistently appropriate register, and excellent sense of purpose and audience. ***Development of ideas:*** Shows independence of thought. Ideas are well developed, at appropriate length and persuasive. Quality is sustained throughout. Enjoyable to read. The interest of the reader is aroused and sustained.	8–9	**Fluent** ***Style:*** Almost first language competence. Ease of style. Confident and wide-ranging use of language, idiom and tenses. ***Accuracy:*** No or very few errors. Well-constructed and linked paragraphs.
6–7	**Effective** ***Relevance:*** Fulfils the task, with appropriate register and good sense of purpose and audience. ***Development of ideas:*** Ideas are well developed and at appropriate length. Engages reader's interest.	6–7	**Precise** ***Style:*** Sentences show variety of structure and length. Some style and turn of phrase. Uses some idioms and is precise in use of vocabulary. However, there may be some awkwardness in style, making reading less enjoyable. ***Accuracy:*** Generally accurate, apart from occasional frustrating minor errors. There are paragraphs showing some unity, although links may be absent or inappropriate.
4–5	**Satisfactory** ***Relevance:*** Fulfils the task, with reasonable attempt at appropriate register, and some sense of purpose and audience. A satisfactory attempt has been made to address the topic, but there may be digressions. ***Development of ideas:*** Material is satisfactorily developed at appropriate length.	4–5	**Safe** ***Style:*** Mainly simple structures and vocabulary, sometimes attempting more sophisticated language. ***Accuracy:*** Meaning is clear, and work is of a safe, literate standard. Simple structures are generally sound, apart from infrequent spelling errors, which do not interfere with communication. Grammatical errors occur when more sophistication is attempted. Paragraphs are used but without coherence or unity.
2–3	**Partly relevant** ***Relevance:*** Partly relevant and some engagement with the task. Does not quite fulfil the task, although there are some positive qualities. Inappropriate register, showing insufficient awareness of purpose and/or audience. ***Development of ideas:*** Supplies some detail and explanation, but the effect is incomplete. Some repetition.	2–3	**Errors intrude** ***Style:*** Simple structures and vocabulary. ***Accuracy:*** Meaning is sometimes in doubt. Frequent, distracting errors hamper precision and slow down reading. However, these do not seriously impair communication. Paragraphs absent or inconsistent.
0–1	**Little relevance** Limited engagement with the task, but this is mostly hidden by density of error. **(Award 1 mark.)** No engagement with the task, or any engagement with the task is completely hidden by density of error. **(Award 0 marks.)** If essay is completely irrelevant, no mark can be given for language.	0–1	**Hard to understand** Multiple types of error in grammar/spelling/word usage/punctuation throughout which mostly make understanding difficult. Sense can be deciphered occasionally. Paragraphs absent or inconsistent. **(Award 1 mark.)** Density of error completely obscures meaning. Whole sections impossible to recognise as pieces of English writing. Paragraphs absent or inconsistent. **(Award 0 marks.)**

PRACTICE TEST 1

Exercise 1 *[8 marks]*

(a) It is a World Heritage Site.
(b) It was a supply base for soldiers (in the 17 forts) along Hadrian's Wall.
(c) Officers: *Any 2 of:* spacious / luxurious / mosaics (on floors) / courtyards / fountains
Soldiers: *Any 2 of:* cramped / dark / uncomfortable
(d) *Any 2 of*: weapons / armour / jewellery / tombstones / altars
(e) *Any 3 of:* dig / study finds with museum staff / piece together pottery / writing
(f) 3.30 p.m.
(g) 10 minutes

Exercise 2 *[14 marks]*

(a) It has good camouflage / Its colours are forest colours/shadowy and dark/adapted to its environment.
(b) (i) shy / avoid each other
(ii) spread out over a wide area
(c) They dig pits (with the help of Mbuti trackers).
(d) (i) She hides it from other animals.
(ii) She returns 2 or 3 times a day to nurse it.
(e) They have increased the scale of hunting.
(f) The scale of their hunting is not destructive.
(g) in the north(-east) of the Democratic Republic of Congo
(h) The forest eco-system has been disturbed/damaged.
(i) *Any 4 of:*
- Learn more about them.
- End conflicts in the region.
- Protect the forest/their habitat.
- Stop clearing nearby areas for farming.
- Reduce/stop illegal hunting.
- Work with wildlife agencies.
- Get the support of the government.
- Protect the National Parks.

Exercise 3 *[8 marks]*

See completed form on page 89.

Exercise 4 *[8 marks]*

The protein found in some residents' blood

Any 2 of:
- Makes them immune to heart disease.
- Called 'apolipoprotein A1 Milano-Limone'.
- Carried by 235 people/by descendants of a couple who married in 1644.

Tourism in Limone

Any 2 of:
- Nearly a million tourists between March and November each year.
- 4,000 tourists/4 times the town's population per day.
- Now more important than lemon growing.

Geographical location

- On Lake Garda in northern Italy.
- Surrounded by mountains (which protect it from winter cold).

The history of lemon growing

Any 2 of:
- Lemons brought to Europe from the Middle East/in the 12th century.
- Used to treat many illnesses (typhoid/malaria/migraine/rheumatism).
- 15 million produced annually in Limone in 19th century.
- Grown in 'limonaiae'/frames.

Exercise 5 *[10 marks]*

Content

One mark for each correct point, up to 6 marks.

How Fairtrade benefits small farmers

- Prevents them falling into debt/losing their livelihood.
- Guarantees they get a fair price, whatever the world situation.
- better/more stable future for farmer and family
- They can build their own houses.
- Their children can go to school.
- Labels products so consumers know they can help.
- Provides regular income.
- (Fairtrade premium) provides sanitation/water.
- subsidised meals
- Helps local sports teams.

Language

Up to 4 marks. Use the table on page 82 as a guide.

Model summary

Fairtrade makes sure that small-scale farmers receive fair payment for their crops, regardless of fluctuating world prices. Farmers and their families have a more stable future as a result of this regular income; they are able to build their own houses and educate their children. Farmers receive a 'premium' in addition to the guaranteed price and this has funded community projects such as sanitation, clean water and subsidised canteens. It has even enabled farmers to provide local sports teams with uniforms and equipment. The Fairtrade label means that consumers can help the farmers by choosing to buy Fairtrade goods. *(99 words)*

Exercise 6 *[18 marks]*

Content and language

Up to 9 marks for each. Use the table on page 83 as a guide.

A model composition is provided on page 94.

Exercise 7 *[18 marks]*

Content and language

Up to 9 marks for each. Use the table on page 83 as a guide.
A model composition is provided on page 94.

PRACTICE TEST 2

Exercise 1 *[8 marks]*

(a) remote quarry on edge of (Snowdonia) National Park *(both points needed)*
(b) to try out new alternative technologies / to find solutions to the world's energy problems
(c) Because many of the ideas are now common practice.
(d) saving on household energy costs
(e) water
(f) flowers growing on (turf) roofs
(g) eco-adventure playground; workshops (where they can design models) *(both points needed)*
(h) by arriving by bicycle

Exercise 2 *[14 marks]*

(a) He heard their (characteristic) 'hoo-hooing' sound.
(b) He was fascinated by their habits.
(c) They are very big (in relation to the weight of the bird).
(d) Their size makes it difficult for them to fly among trees.
(e) 142 cm
(f) They direct sound towards their ears (so they can locate hidden prey).
(g) He continues hunting when visibility is bad/during a snowstorm.
(h) *Any 2 of:*
- She shreds food and drops it into their mouths.
- She will starve herself to make sure they get as much food as possible.
- She protects them on the ground (after they have left the nest).

(i) *Any 4 of:*
- They fly silently.
- Their knife-sharp beaks.
- They are very powerful.
- They can dive through snow crust/frozen snow.
- They can snatch prey hidden under the snow.

(j) Because the nest develops a smell which makes it obvious to predators.

Exercise 3 *[8 marks]*

See completed form on page 90.

Exercise 4 *[8 marks]*

Origins and purpose of Silbo Gomero

- Brought by settlers/from North Africa.
- Developed for long-distance communication.

Features of the language

Any 3 of:
- Sounds like birdsong.
- Uses Spanish speech patterns.
- Uses tones (not vowels and consonants).
- Is whistled at different frequencies.
- Has over 4,000 words.

Why the language was disappearing

Any 1 of:
- arrival of the telephone/modern technology
- contact with tourists/the outside world
- Islanders felt embarrassed/thought it was primitive.

How the language is being revived

Any 2 of:
- Children are learning it at school.
- Research is being done in places where Gomerans emigrated/where the language survives.
- The government hopes to attract outside support.

Exercise 5 *[10 marks]*

Content

One mark for each correct point, up to 6 marks.

How becoming a teacher changed Baldev Singh's life and the lives of his pupils

- Left a well-paid job.
- Stopped working on his own (in a laboratory).
- Travelled to Cairo, Jordan and South Africa.
- Became interested in IT.
- Made links with schools in India & South Africa.
- Became Head of the IT department.
- Pupils became more motivated.
- They developed skills in a more meaningful/practical way.
- They used the internet to collaborate with pupils in India & South Africa.

Language

Up to 4 marks. Use the table on page 82 as a guide.

Model summary

Baldev used to be well paid but, since becoming a school teacher, he enjoys being with people instead of working alone in a university lab. He became interested in using IT to teach citizenship and has travelled to Cairo, Jordan and South Africa with his work. He has even helped to train police cadets abroad. Using IT has made his pupils more motivated and interested in their school work, by allowing them to develop skills in a meaningful way. They now use the internet to collaborate and exchange information with schools in India and South Africa. Baldev has become Head of IT and loves his work. *(106 words)*

Exercise 6 *[18 marks]*

Content and language

Up to 9 marks for each. Use the table on page 83 as a guide.
A model composition is provided on page 94.

Exercise 7 *[18 marks]*

Content and language

Up to 9 marks for each. Use the table on page 83 as a guide.
A model composition is provided on page 95.

PRACTICE TEST 3

Exercise 1 *[8 marks]*

(a) fat, sugar and salt
(b) (i) Levels of fat, sugar and salt have been reduced in 1000 products.
(ii) Levels are being reduced in 950 more products.
(c) They provide clear nutritional information/a nutritional breakdown of each product.
(d) at-a-glance / easy-to-read
(e) Guideline Daily Amounts / GDAs
(f) website: www.foodlabels.com/health
(g) 19
(h) The shopper can mix healthy and less healthy foods and stay within the recommended daily amounts.

Exercise 2 *[14 marks]*

(a) to improve the health of children/young people/the next generation
(b) drawing and designing using computers and conventional materials
(c) They are concerned about growing obesity and related diseases in the young.
(d) They explain the Games clearly / They explain in language children can understand / They explain in language suited to the age group.
(e) She is a wheelchair user.
(f) the opportunity to travel
(g) They are unaware of the variety of sports available.
(h) They are suitable for the weather / They are nationally supported.
(i) Spain
(j) football
(k) *Any 4 of:*
fair play / respect for others / teamwork / the desire to win / confidence / ability to handle stress / self-respect

Exercise 3 *[8 marks]*

See completed form on page 91.

Exercise 4 *[8 marks]*

Babylonian economy based on

Any 2 of:

- agriculture

- foreign trade
- manufactured goods / textiles

Language

- Akkadian
- cuneiform system of writing

Scientific achievements

Any 2 of

- Invented system of weights and measures (later used by Greeks and Romans).
- Excelled at mathematics.
- surgery (including eye operations)

Religion in Babylonian society

Any 1 of:

- Each city had own god or goddess.
- Bel/Marduk king of gods/god of city of Babylon
- elaborate daily rituals at the temples

Social organisation

- king with absolute power

Exercise 5 *[10 marks]*

Content

One mark for each correct point, up to 6 marks.
For full marks, both aspects of the question must be covered.

Why the students are keen to go to the Indian Institute of Technology

- elite/prestigious institute
- fame
- success
- get a good degree

What they need to do to prepare

- Study at a special educational academy.
- Put up with heat/discomfort/overcrowding.
- Take 2 3-hour exams.
- If fail, try again.
- Study for very long hours.
- Remain optimistic.

Language

Up to 4 marks. Use the table on page 82 as a guide.

Model summary

Students are so keen to go to the Indian Institute of Technology because it is a very prestigious place to study and they have a good chance of getting an excellent degree there. In addition, they may achieve fame and success like some of the famous past students.

They have to work very hard to prepare. First they need to go to a small educational academy for special intensive coaching, enduring overcrowding, and even standing in very high temperatures to hear the teachers. If they subsequently fail the exams, they try again and remain optimistic while they continue to study for very long hours. *(104 words)*

Exercise 6 *[18 marks]*

Content and language

Up to 9 marks for each. Use the table on page 83 as a guide.
A model composition is provided on page 95.

Exercise 7 *[18 marks]*

Content and language

Up to 9 marks for each. Use the table on page 83 as a guide.
A model composition is provided on page 95.

PRACTICE TEST 4

Exercise 1 *[8 marks]*

(a) There's something for all the family.
(b) They can push (coloured) buttons and watch what happens.
(c) (i) To show the problem of disposing of old mobile phones. (ii) To show how cartoons are made.
(d) (i) walking on the Moon
(ii) searching for wild animals
(e) It has won an award.
(f) by visiting the museum's website (www.sciencemuseum.org)
(g) use of flashing lights (in some exhibits)

Exercise 2 *[14 marks]*

(a) to symbolise a place where plants/ideas grow
(b) granite, one of the world's toughest rocks
(c) 167 tonnes
(d) its domes/biomes
(e) *Any 2 of:* buildings / webcams / video recordings / geographical features
(f) It blooms for 48 hours and then dies.

(g) To show plants which have changed the world.
(h) It has been called the 8th Wonder of the World / More than 10 million people have visited it.
(i) *All 4 of:*
- Has transformed empty clay pits into fertile land.
- Encourages thinking about future possibilities for the environment.
- Raises awareness / Educates visitors about global environment.
- Uses renewable energy.

Exercise 3 *[8 marks]*

See completed form on page 92.

Exercise 4 *[8 marks]*

Location of the village of Oymyakon

Any 2 of:
- north-eastern Siberia
- 200 miles south of the Arctic Circle
- (6000 feet up) in the Verkhoyansk mountains

How homes are adapted to the climate

Any 3 of:
- built of wood (rather than stone)
- no plumbing
- lavatory in an outhouse
- water kept in blocks of ice outside
- storage room for fish and meat under the house

Traditional diet

Any 3 of:
- meat
- fish
- mushrooms
- berries

Exercise 5 *[10 marks]*

Content

One mark for each correct point, up to 6 marks.
For full marks, both aspects of the question must be covered.

Physical characteristics and behaviour of bats

- wing like a hand
- size of a plum
- light in weight / weight of 10 paperclips
- sharp teeth
- hunt at night using echo-location
- catch insects with their feet

How declining bat populations can be helped

- scented night plants/trees/ponds to attract insects
- trees for roosting sites
- bat boxes (on trees/walls)
- protection by law
- provision of alternative roosting sites if disturbed
- protection groups gathering information/promoting public awareness/educating the public

Language

Up to 4 marks. Use the table on page 82 as a guide.

Model summary

Bats or 'flying mice' are small and light (weighing no more than ten paperclips). They use their sharp teeth to feed on insects, fruit, blood, fish or even other bats, depending on the species. Many use echo-location to hunt at night, catching insects with their feet. Endangered bats are helped by the provision of scented plants, trees and ponds, to attract insects. Bat boxes for roosting can also help, and alternative sites can be provided if a bat colony is disturbed. Protection groups can gather information and educate the public about bats and how to care for them.
(98 words)

Exercise 6 *[18 marks]*

Content and language

Up to 9 marks for each. Use the table on page 83 as a guide.
A model composition is provided on page 96.

Exercise 7 *[18 marks]*

Up to 9 marks for each. Use the table on page 83 as a guide.
A model composition is provided on page 96.

The Ten Hills Challenge

– raising funds for research into cancer

PARTICIPANTS' APPLICATION FORM

SECTION A

Name (in BLOCK CAPITALS): NADIA VAN DEN BROK

Date of birth: 3.7.88

Occupation: Student

Country of residence: India

Full address: Bungalow 4, Block 11, Kalyan Road, Bombay

Email address: nvandenbrok@aol.com

Emergency contact number (family member, please): 07703 987 765

SECTION B

Dates available for training: Last week of January

Which language should the trainer use for you? (please tick)

☐ Hindi ☑ English ☐ Other (please state): ______

Preferred dates for actual Ten Hill Challenge (please circle):

March 30–April 1 (April 4–6)

Accommodation type preferred: Youth hostel

Please specify any special dietary requirements: Vegetarian

SECTION C

Write one sentence of **12–20 words** explaining how you intend to raise funds to enter the Ten Hills Challenge.

Our group will organise a garden party with musical entertainment, and my college will match the amount raised.

Test 1, Exercise 3 [Total: 8]

ONLINE SHOPPING EVALUATION FORM

Section A

(Block capitals, please, for name and home address.)

Name of the person completing this form: JAMIE MORAN

Home address: 145 DUNE STREET, CORK 17, REPUBLIC OF IRELAND

Email address: moranj@ecomail.com

Male / ~~Female~~ *(Delete)*

How many people live in your household? Adults [3] Children under 18 [3]

Section B

How long have you been using the internet to shop for goods or services? *(Please tick)*

0–12 months ☐ 1–2 years ☑ 2–3 years ☐ 3–5 years ☐ More than 5 years ☐

What have been the benefits of online shopping for you or anyone in your household? *Tick any relevant statements below.*

Goods are cheaper ☐

Wider range of choice for a particular product ☐

Used/second-hand goods available ☐

Easier to compare prices of products ☐

More convenient form of shopping ☑

Unusual or hard-to-find items available ☑

More anonymous way to shop ☐

Have you or anyone in your household been disappointed with online shopping services? (Yes) / No *(Please circle)*

If yes, please tick any relevant statements below.

Poor quality of goods ☐

Wrong price charged ☑

Wrong quantity supplied ☐

Goods broken or damaged on arrival ☐

Goods not as expected ☑

Goods arrived late ☐

Poor fit ☑

Have you, or any member of your household, ever made a complaint about any good/services bought online? (Yes) / No *(Please circle)*

If yes, what was the nature of the complaint? Overcharged for the item purchased

Section C

We are interested in finding out whether online shopping is likely to replace high street shopping in the future. Write a sentence of **between 12 and 20 words** giving your opinion.

I doubt it, as people find high street shopping enjoyable and like handling things before buying.

APPLICATION FORM: MUSICAL EXCELLENCE AWARD

SECTION A: CONTACT DETAILS

Name: Andrea Tomas — Age: 16

Telephone: 07779 683259 — E-mail: atomas@yahoo.com

Bank code: 42-70-11 — Account number: 93537352

Availability during award audition period: 4th 5th (6th) (7th) 8th June (*please circle as many days as possible*)

For applicants under 18 years, please supply names of parents/guardians:

Simon and Hazel Tomas

SECTION B: RELEVANT MUSICAL EXPERIENCE

Main instrument: clarinet

Level of achievement: Performance Diploma

Other musical instruments/abilities: piano and singing

Positions of responsibility held: Leader of clarinet section/4 other clarinetists (in regional Junior Orchestra)

SECTION C: FURTHER DETAILS

If successful in obtaining an award, I wish to learn with :

Mrs Schmidt (*supply name of preferred teacher*)

I confirm that I am able to attend next year's spring residential course, from 6 – 12 April:

YES NO (*delete as necessary*)

Names and status of two referees:

1) Name: Mrs Schmidt — Status: clarinet teacher

2) Name: Mr Braun — Status: choir director

SECTION D

In the space below, write **one sentence of between 12 and 20 words** giving details of any relevant future plans.

I hope to study music at university and then become conductor of an orchestra, after following a specialist postgraduate course.

Test 3, Exercise 3 [Total: 8]

GREETINGS INTERNATIONAL VOLUNTEER GROUP

Tour guide application form

(Please write your name and address in CAPITALS.)

PART A

Name: SHIRAZ MALAWI

Age: 17 Male / ~~Female~~ (*please delete*)

Address: 3500 PUTTALAM AVENUE,
COLOMBO, SRI LANKA

Telephone number: 0094-216-6790925

Email address: smalawi@yahoo.com

PART B

Name of school or college: Sri Lanka Main School

Languages studied and level of proficiency: French & Spanish (GCSE), English & Italian (A-level)

PART C

Preferred placement location (*please circle one*):

Africa Americas Asia Australasia Europe

Available month (*please circle one*):

May June July August September January February

PART D

Please provide details of 2 relevant referees:

1) Name: Mr A. Malik

Institution and position held:
Head, Sri Lanka Main School, Colombo

2) Name: Mr B. Premadasa

Institution and position held:
Curator, Local History Museum, Sea Road, Colombo

PART E

Please write one sentence of **12–20 words** explaining why you feel you are a suitable candidate to be a GREETINGS volunteer.

My language knowledge and museum experience will help me to guide and inform people as they visit historic places.

Test 4, Exercise 3 [Total: 8]

Model compositions

PRACTICE TEST 1

Exercise 6 *(page 28)*

(Dear Emil,)

Just a quick line to tell you what has been happening here.

My uncle has been manager of a toy factory for twenty years and he retired last week. His company gave a big party for him, to thank him and celebrate his retirement. Family members were invited too.

Unfortunately, on the way to the party another car crashed into us! We had stopped to let a woman with a pushchair cross the road, another car came round the corner too fast and the driver couldn't stop in time. Luckily, no-one was hurt – just a bit shaken. I'm glad I was wearing my seat belt, I can tell you! However, the back of Dad's car was really smashed up. The driver reluctantly agreed to pay for the damage and we continued our journey by taxi.

We arrived at the party to the sound of cheering as my uncle went onto the platform to make his retirement speech. We were so glad we made it in time.

Write to me soon and let me know all your news.
(177 words)

Exercise 7 *(page 30)*

(Dear Editor,)

I am writing to express my support for your campaign for a post office in our village. At the moment, residents have to travel several kilometres to buy stamps, to post or collect parcels and to obtain licences or passport forms; it will help us all to be able to do these things locally.

The new post office will also bring modern technology to our village. Access to information on the internet will help us all, and being able to use email will benefit our communication skills. In addition, this new business will create at least eight new jobs in the village.

Some people who live near the intended post office site are worried about the noise of the constant rush of customers during business hours. Some are also concerned that people using the post office will leave rubbish behind and damage the environment. However, these disadvantages can be managed by employing sufficient post office staff to cope efficiently with high numbers of customers.

The benefits of the new post office will far outweigh the possible problems. In my view, our local community should recognise the need for this business and give you full support in your campaign.

(Yours faithfully,) *(198 words)*

PRACTICE TEST 2

Exercise 6 *(page 44)*

I would like to nominate my Information Technology teacher Mr Banda for the Outstanding Teacher Award.

He has taught us for five years and we know so much more about the World Wide Web, as well as how to use all kinds of software, because of his teaching. This now makes our studies so much easier. We can all now produce excellent work for our other classes because our computer skills have improved so much. Our other teachers have noticed the improvement.

The award should be given to Mr Banda because he is special and he never gets angry or impatient with us, no matter how many times we ask him for help. He has a really clear way of making complicated things seem very simple. Sometimes he will stay late with us so we can finish a project or understand some difficult ideas.

We all feel he likes us and wants us to do well and get good grades in our exams. Mr Banda always goes that extra mile for us, so I think we should show him how much we appreciate him by giving him this award. *(189 words)*

Exercise 7 *(page 46)*

Each day, thousands of people are inspired by a visit to a place of interest, or a programme about history, or a book or picture linked with a historical event. Souvenirs, postcards and photographs all remind us of our own historical experiences.

We all need to think why history matters. It can, for example, be a lesson learned and an insurance against a repeat of disastrous events. To promote the 'History Matters' campaign, the organisers want everyone to send in a few lines about why history matters to them. They ask you to step away from iPods, email and mobile phones for just a few minutes and consider the importance of history.

History, of course, is not just about the past – it also has to do with the future. What do we retain that was here a hundred years ago and will still be here in another hundred years? History is culture and civilisation – it is mankind, and each individual.

It needs to be kept alive, valued and respected, and passed on from generation to generation, so that our grandchildren may have the same wonderful experiences of their heritage that our great-grandparents had in their own youth. Our history matters – pass it on! *(203 words)*

PRACTICE TEST 3

Exercise 6 *(page 60)*

(Dear Lili,)

My family and I are really looking forward to your visit. We are hoping that the weather will be good so we can do lots of things.

You'll need to bring clothes for warm weather and a raincoat just in case it rains. Apart from that we can provide everything else you might need.

There are so many things to do here. First of all we'll show you our town. It's quite small so it's easy to find your way around, and there are some interesting shops. Maybe we can take a picnic to the Castle Park. It has lovely gardens with a boating lake where we can hire a boat if you like. If the weather is too hot we can go inside the Castle Museum, which explains the history of the town right up to the present day.

Some things are very different from your country. For a start the weather is very changeable and the roads are always busy. You might notice the care almost everyone takes with their small but colourful gardens at this time of year.

We hope that you are going to have a wonderful time with us. Have a safe journey. *(198 words)*

Exercise 7 *(page 62)*

(Dear Editor,)

As I see it, adding folic acid to bread is a good development. We have lots of unhealthy additives in our food, so why should we worry about this vitamin being added when it is good for us? The label on some white bread in shops says bleach is one of the ingredients, which is much worse for our health.

Some readers are concerned that the government is interfering in our lives and trying to control us. I don't agree, as you are still free to make your own bread if you want to. I also believe that adding this vitamin could help people who don't like green vegetables, or can't afford them, to be healthier.

Furthermore, the suggestion that we don't know what folic acid in bread would do to our long-term health is ridiculous. No-one knows exactly how food will affect us eventually, as nothing in the future is guaranteed; but experts have done scientific trials to show this idea is reasonably safe.

I know many of your readers will still be making their minds up about this. I hope reading my views will help persuade them that this development will benefit us all. *(196 words)*

PRACTICE TEST 4

Exercise 6 *(page 76)*

I am 16 years old and what I enjoy about being the age I am now is all the exciting opportunities that are ahead of me. Although I haven't made up my mind what I want to do in the future, it doesn't worry me. I think there are many choices available and all my options are still open.

What many of my friends and I find difficult is the fact that at our age we don't have much money of our own. If I had a lot of money I'd buy a DVD player for the whole family, as we love watching films. Also, when you don't have money you can't help others. I'd like to pay off my parents' mortgage or buy them more land for our farm, but I can't.

What is the best age to be? I'm not sure. I loved being younger, as I could play all day, but I'm also looking forward to being 24. Around that age I will have finished college and will perhaps have started in a good career. I might be able to do some of the things I have always dreamed of, like travelling and seeing the world.
(199 words)

Exercise 7 *(page 78)*

(Dear Director,)

In my opinion it's about time our local museum improved its facilities.

Whenever I have visited the museum, it has been hard to find my way around and I had to ask the attendants. In addition it is often hard to see what the exhibits actually are, as the lighting is so poor. I think brighter lighting and a clear plan or map would really help everyone to find and enjoy the exhibits.

I also think the museum should think about becoming more interactive and letting people touch and experience the exhibits, in order to get to know at first hand what they are all about. In more modern museums you can actually use some of the things on display, which helps you to understand how people lived in the past.

If school groups and students come to the museum they need tables and chairs to work properly, which aren't provided at the moment. In my opinion it wouldn't cost too much for these.

Finally, could we get the bus company to stop right outside the museum? This would encourage many more people to come, especially those who find it difficult to walk. *(193 words)*

www.ingramcontent.com/pod-product-compliance
Ingram Content Group UK Ltd.
Pitfield, Milton Keynes, MK11 3LW, UK
UKHW060611180726
13836UKWH00011B/2505

* 9 7 8 0 5 2 1 1 4 0 6 5 2 *